Where in the
WORLD
is GOD?

Where in the WORLD is GOD?

God's Presence in Every Moment of Our Lives

Foreword by John B. Cobb, Jr.

Robert Brizee

THE UPPER ROOM
Nashville, Tennessee

Where in the World Is God?

Book and Cover Design: Roy Wallace
First Printing: June 1987 (5)
Library of Congress Catalogue Card Number: 86-051152
ISBN: 0-8358-0556-5

Printed in the United States of America

DEDICATION

Lovingly dedicated to Adrienne,
who heard it all in process

Contents

Foreword

WHERE in the world is God? During the past two centuries this question has become a quite serious one. The "modern" world view began in seeing God as the cause of everything and ended in pushing God out of the world altogether. Natural law changed from being the law imposed on the world by God to being the way nature worked without God. On the way, there was a big argument about whether there were events that violated natural law and therefore expressed God's direct activity in the world. We are still heirs of all those eighteenth-and-nineteenth-century ideas, but they are less and less convincing.

So, where in the world is God? For a great many people, even church people, the honest answer seems to be "nowhere." Everything that happens seems to belong to the world that is fully explained by natural and historical causes. If God is God anywhere at all, it must be somewhere else, somewhere very transcendent, somewhere that has very little connection with the world in which we live.

Others are sure this is wrong. They have had, or know of

9

others having had, extraordinary experiences—mystical experiences, experiences of presence, answers to prayer, feelings of the sacred, transformations through faith — that convince them that God is sometimes present in the world or that human beings can somehow meet God at the boundaries of the world.

Others find God in the church. Sometimes it is in the human fellowship they find there. Sometimes it is in the music. Sometimes it is in the sacraments. Sometimes it is in the preached word. Because they meet God in the church, they know that God is present also in the world even though they do not discern God's presence there so keenly.

Others see the hand of God in the great events of history. They find in the Bible a way of interpreting events that makes sense of war and peace, of Auschwitz and the State of Israel, of prosperity and depression. They see the meaning of individual lives as bound up in this sweep of history.

Others find God in the sheer existence of things. What happens in the course of events may be explained, for them, by natural causes. But the being of things, that is, their own existence, is pure mystery. It points to God as the giver of all being, as Being Itself.

Others understand that whatever happens is what God does. By God, they mean the totality or that which wholly controls the totality. There can be nothing at all that is not the doing of this totality or this one power determining all things.

Still others discern God in and through everything that happens but do not identify what God does as all that happens. They find God lovingly and creatively present and at work in every event, but what happens is never due to God alone. God was present at Auschwitz, strengthening the inmates in their endurance, encouraging the humanity of their treatment one of another, and supporting their continuing faith in the meaning of life when all the external signs pointed to its meaninglessness. God suffered with them in their suffering. But God was not the torturer or executioner.

The answer of process theology to the question Where in the world is God? belongs to this final family of answers. In the philosophy of Alfred North Whitehead, it finds a highly technical, thoroughly contemporary account of what God is doing in the events that make up the world. The discussion is difficult to follow, but the implications for practical Christian life are vivid and important.

For years, Dr. Robert Brizee has been teaching and counseling in terms of what he has learned from Whitehead about where God is in the world. He has learned how to take this abstruse conceptuality and interpret everyday life by its help. Those who have been trying for years to teach these ideas know that this is no small achievement.

Of course, not everyone will agree. Those who believe that God calls all the shots are likely to complain that the God Brizee presents is too "limited." The much more numerous group who have banished God from ordinary affairs altogether may complain that they want to keep God for special occasions or maintain a much greater distance. But for millions of ordinary Christians who believe that, in the Holy Spirit and the living Christ, God is a creative presence in their lives but who are confused as to just how to think of that presence, Brizee's book can be an illuminating and inspiring opportunity to think and see more clearly.

How we understand God and how we understand ourselves go together, and every authentic discipline of spiritual formation must express that understanding. Seeing better

11

who we are in relation to God's call and empowerment can ground and guide our practice of prayer and meditation. May the reader find God in a convincing way and find also the way to be more fully directed and empowered by the Holy Spirit!

JOHN B. COBB, JR.

Preface

*T*ODAY many of us desire to have a rich relationship with God, yet we do not know how to do so. We attempt prayer but falter. We study the traditional spiritual disciplines but do not feel at home with them. The desire is strong; the way is unclear.

I believe that much of our difficulty lies with how we think about God. The way we think of God leads us to images of how God relates to us, which in turn lead us to ways of forming a relationship. Thinking leads to imagining, which leads to practice.

I have addressed this book to those of us who are searching. It presents the Caring Friend as a new way of picturing how God is present with us. Starting with this image, we can develop new ways of opening and enriching a relationship with God.

The first section of the book poses the question in the lives of six ordinary people: Where in the world is God? For them, God must be somewhere doing something but does not appear to be with them. The second section offers an answer by presenting the new image of Caring Friend. The third illustrates the lively activity of God in a variety of both ordinary and dramatic human events. All of the events grow out of my own experiences or those of people I know.

I am a stagehand. My job is to set the stage so that plays may be performed. I set the stage and offer some of my own dramas. Most importantly, however, I invite you to begin to act out your own dramas on the stage I am setting.

This book is truly a "tale of two cities"! It was created from the abundant contributions of the adult class at the First United Methodist Church of Wenatchee, Washington, and the Process and Faith steering committee at the School of Theology at Claremont, California. The class prompted me to make the ideas easy to understand and relevant to daily life, while the committee kept me true to the theology being interpreted. I am grateful to both for their encircling caring and creative influence in shaping this book. I acknowledge especially the caring of Dr. John B. Cobb, Jr., and Dr. William A. Beardslee in their mentor role of suggesting, guiding, encouraging, and consoling. Their personal graciousness reflects their theology.

I am indebted to Ms. Lynn Brown for suggesting the title for the book; to Gil and Myrtle Manor for offering their lake cottage for many hours of early morning writing; to Ms. Aneyth Baker, the mother of my wife, Adrienne, for her loving trust in our marriage and what we might accomplish together; and to Rabbi Harold Kushner for asking our committee the provoking question which influenced me to reshape the entire book: What questions are people out there asking which you have come together here to answer?

For typing the manuscript, I thank Ms. Sally DeMarce for the first draft and Ms. Jeanne Peterson for the final draft. I have deep appreciation to my wife, Adrienne, for reading countless paragraphs and chapters, many of which never made it beyond her discerning eyes.

Finally, I must witness to my mysterious experience with the One about whom I wrote, who lured me time and again to go beyond the limit of what I thought I could do to a higher vision of what was possible. I am grateful for experiencing in the very process of writing that about which I wrote!

I.

RAISING THE QUESTION:

Where in the World Is God?

1.

Where Is God?

SUE awoke as she had so many mornings to the singing of the robins in the maple tree near her bedroom window. It was a familiar and soothing sound. Streaks of sunlight outlined the drawn shade. A gentle breeze caused a slight swaying of the curtain. She felt good.

Then a knot tightened in her stomach as she was jolted back to reality. Tom is gone! It wasn't simply a bad dream the morning sunlight would chase away. Tom had died. Tears welled up and flowed down her cheek onto the pillow. How many times had she forgotten, only to be shocked again by the stark, bleak fact?

Yesterday was largely a blur: friends in suits and ties; dresses and heels; large, shiny cars; sweet-smelling flowers; sad faces, tears, and hugs; organ music; hard, wooden pews; words, words, words; friends awkwardly carrying the gray metal casket; the smell of the new-mown grass at the cemetery; and wobbly knees and sick stomach as it was time to turn and leave for good.

Remembering was unbearable. The pain was too much.

A part of her had been ripped away. It was nearly two years since they had started to go steady. After all he had been through with her, then in an instant to be gone!

But the unanswered questions were just as unbearable. Why? Why Tom? A good person, a junior in high school, he was just beginning his life. If he had been reckless and always tempting fate, maybe it would make more sense. So far, nothing made sense.

She did recall, in spite of the blur of yesterday, the words from the sermon: "God needed Tom." In God's realm, the minister said, there was a task that only Tom could accomplish, so God took Tom. She remembered feeling the hair on the back of her neck bristle and her fists clench as she listened. There was no way that she could imagine God doing that.

What could be more important than her being with Tom? What could possibly be more important than a young man in the prime of his life living to the fullest? And what does taking Tom say about God's love for her? Would God's desire come first without regard for what this ripping away would do to her?

While Sue disagreed violently with the answer given at the funeral, she did not have a better one for herself. She was clear what she rejected, but not clear what she believed. The questions kept swirling in her head. Why? Why Tom? Why so young? Why me?

Her thoughts drew her back once again to the accident. If only Tom had slowed down his bike on the curve . . . but he didn't. But then, why didn't God step in? Where was God when the accident was happening? Couldn't God have done something to prevent it or at least to keep it from being so bad?

After all, didn't God create everything? Don't people

pray to Almighty God? Doesn't the psalm say that God is like a shepherd to the flock? Isn't the Bible filled with miracles? What do you have to do to qualify for a miracle? So why wasn't something done for Tom? Where was God when Tom needed God? Where is God now when I need God?

Walt was up early that Sunday morning. He always liked to get up, have a small glass of orange juice, and read the Portland *Oregonian* while Marian slept in. He stepped outside and lightly touched the patio railing, which he had painted the day before. It was their place, totally paid for. He had retired just one month ago today. Life tasted good! He leafed leisurely through the pages of the newspaper, enjoying the sounds of the Toutle River just below his patio.

The date was May 18, 1980. At 8:32 that morning, a shattering blast occurred as Mount St. Helens erupted. A plume of smoke ten miles high belched forth; tons of ash were thrown throughout the state of Washington; twelve hundred feet of mountain were blown away; over fifty persons died, buried beneath the ash or killed instantly by the searing heat.

The beautiful Spirit Lake was torn and mangled; massive snowfields were melted, sending torrents of water cascading downward; thousands of animals were incinerated; tall, lush evergreens were left standing like matchsticks; wildflowers were decimated; millions of fish in the rivers were boiled in the steaming brown water; and the contours of the rivers and countryside at lower elevations were reshaped like a child drawing a stick through a mud puddle. That part of Washington State was declared a disaster area.

Walt and Marian were not allowed to return to their home after the evacuation. However, they did hear reports from authorities at the scene that the river bank upon which

21

their home stood no longer existed. Their home was one of a number seen floating on the raging river until dashed into oblivion by the rapids. The news left them numb.

Like a puff of smoke, their dream home, the result of innumerable weekends and evenings, vanished. Their life savings, their furniture, the picture albums and scrapbooks, the bronzed baby shoes, the last few cherished belongings of their parents, their clothes, and the land itself perished.

It was, of course, a natural disaster, not one shaped by human hands. They were grateful to still be alive, for many had been killed. Still, they could not help but ask why. Why at this point in their lives was their future devastated? What sense did it make? What meaning did it have?

They felt shock, confusion, anger, and despair. They had trusted in an orderly world and a just God. They had believed that as they sow so shall they reap. They had played by the rules of life for decades and had lost everything in a mere span of hours.

Had they not worked hard, raised three fine children, been honest and responsible citizens, contributed to worthy causes, been active in their church, and nursed Marian's mother during her declining years? Had they not sacrificed and saved, looking forward to a better day? What had they done to deserve this? Why this, just when they had reached retirement and built a lovely home in a beautiful setting?

It just didn't seem fair. Their orderly world was thrown into chaos. Confusion reigned. Where was God in the midst of this disaster?

It was a hot summer afternoon. Three eleven-year-old boys pushed their bicycles toward a fast-food restaurant, looking forward to a cool drink. Seconds later, all three were sprawled on the ground, two dead and one wounded by rifle fire. The surviving boy lay still, playing dead, singing softly to himself. The boys were victims of a twenty-one-person massacre, all shot down by one gunman.

Juan, a classmate of the boys, heard about it from a neighborhood friend. After accusing the boy of lying, he jumped on his bicycle and raced to the intersection near the restaurant. The red and blue flashing lights on the police cars and the ambulances standing nearby were all Juan needed to know his friend had told the truth. Tears overwhelmed him as he rushed home.

Flying into the arms of his mother, her hands dripping with soapy dish water, Juan blurted out the news. "It isn't fair, Mom, it isn't fair! What did they ever do to that guy? Why would he shoot them for no reason? How could he do it? They were minding their own business and not bothering anybody! They wouldn't hurt a fly! It isn't right! Why didn't somebody stop him? Why didn't God?"

Blinding tears, loud sobs, and choked voice punctuated the searing questions he hurled at his mother. In his writhing pain, Juan was pleading for justice. Behind his pleading was an unspoken belief in a world that is fair and a God who is just. His mother was faced with a most difficult task. She would search for words that could explain and comfort. The question of an eleven-year-old rings out. How does a God of justice allow injustice?

Sarah decided to say it straight to the callers. She knew they were the church committee that calls on inactive members. She smiled to herself because, years ago, she had been on that very committee. After putting them off twice, she considered trying church again merely to please them but later decided that it was time to be honest with them. She told herself that she would be pleasant but candid.

After the greetings and pleasantries, Sarah told them her story. For over twenty-five years, she had been active in her church, attending worship regularly, teaching church school, serving on the finance committee, presiding over the women's society, and chairing the rummage sale. Church had been important to her and to Bill, her husband, and especially to their son and daughter. Many happy times had been spent with the youth group swimming in their pool and eating popcorn in their family room.

Yet when there was time to look up from all the busy activity, Sarah did not really experience God. She heard others speak of their feelings. She listened to the minister from the pulpit share happenings with God, but she never had such an awareness. There was, of course, the occasional tingly feeling in the back of the neck when the choir concluded an inspiring anthem. There were the awesome moments in the candlelit sanctuary during the Christmas Eve service, but they were the rare exceptions. She had the impression that it never really "took" with her.

On many occasions she struggled with herself, wondering what was wrong with her. Why didn't she experience what others did? Was she lacking something? Was she not trying hard enough?

Then times changed. The children grew up and left home, and later Bill died. Surprisingly, she found that life could go well without church, perhaps even without God. It wasn't that she had changed that much. She still thought of herself as a good person, working in her accounting practice, puttering in the flower garden, golfing, spending occasional weekends at the lake cottage, being the loving grandmother, chairing the local Business and Professional Women's chapter, and volunteering for the yearly United Way campaign.

She missed the people of the church, but in some ways it was a relief not to be there. Now she did not have to go through her inner struggle. She felt more honest now. She did not honestly feel God, hear God, or know God. If God was somewhere, it was clearly not in her daily awareness. If God was around, God must be hidden!

The hands of the round wall clock marked 3:00 A.M. as Ron recorded the final figures on the hourly log chart. He sat at an orderly desk surrounded by panels, dials, radio, telephone, computer screen, and video monitoring system. He mused to himself that the first three hours of the graveyard shift had been quiet and wondered if he might be lucky enough to keep it so. Ron was alone in the Public Utility Building, the power dispatcher in charge.

His curiosity was short-lived. His thoughts were interrupted by a red flashing light on the wall panel. "Oh, oh, trouble near the Greenwood substation!" With near automatic precision, he pulled the switch that stopped the flow of electricity to that vicinity. With one sweeping move, he pressed the automatic dialer on the telephone. This act would bring him into immediate contact with the leader of the repair crew, who was at that moment enjoying a pleasant night's sleep. A sleepy voice answered, and Ron gave directions to stand by.

In the midst of this conversation, a voice blared out from the radio. Accustomed to doing three things at once, Ron grabbed the microphone and responded. It was a police officer at the scene of an accident reporting that a car had crashed into a power pole. Wires were hanging dangerously near the car. Requesting the exact location of the accident, Ron quickly relayed this information to the crew leader.

While Ron was still talking, three incoming lines on the telephone began to flash. He told himself that this would be the public reporting the accident or wondering why their television lost its picture during the late, late movie. Having already given priority to the crucial matters at hand, Ron took each in turn. With the power off and the repair crew on its way, Ron was now ready to do public relations for the district.

In his years, he had handled many frightened and irate people. Step by step, he proceeded. Just as he was taking the third call, the crew leader relayed a report from the scene. Microphone in one hand and telephone in the other, Ron continued. Within twenty minutes, his room was quiet again—another emergency handled well by scientific technology and a rational human being.

Ron thought in the same way that he performed his job. He could handle life well because he knew the system. Life was like one large, complex machine. Actions are planned. Machines work. Results can be predicted. Buttons are pushed, levers are pulled, dials are turned, and things happen.

Machines played a major role in Ron's daily routine. He took his lunch from the refrigerator in his air-conditioned home, touched his automatic garage-door-opener, turned the ignition key of his car, moved the gearshift into reverse, pressed a cassette into the player, pushed the air-conditioner-flow button, and drove with power steering to his office.

On arriving, he placed his plastic identification card into the door monitor and the door clicked to an open position. He took the radio pager from his belt and sat down at his swivel chair.

While at work, Ron knew that the television special that he wanted to see was being recorded on his videocassette recorder. On his way home, he would pick up a few items at the mall where electronic doors open for him. After work, he would mow the lawn with his self-starting, self-propelled power mower. Technology provided convenience, pleasure, and excitement. He would turn to new technology to provide future novelty.

It was clear to him. If trouble develops in a system, find

the malfunction and replace the part, whether it be a battery or a kidney. Life is both predictable and manageable when you know how the machines work. Science had made amazing progress up to now, and even newer machines were just around the corner to make life more convenient and pleasureable.

For Ron, where does God fit in? Frankly, it is hard to find a place. To him the question is more academic than vital. Perhaps God created the universe and the natural laws, but the system runs quite well by itself now. Why does one need God? God doesn't add anything. There is nothing for God to do. Where is God in a world that has no place for God?

Through the voices of Sue, Walt, Marian, Juan, Sarah, and Ron, the question has been raised. Where in the world is God? Though they differ, each person expressed the conviction that if God is to be taken seriously, then God should be somewhere doing something.

2.

God Must Be Somewhere Doing Something

A QUESTION is frequently answered with another question. "Where in the world is God?" "Well, where have you been looking?" Each of the persons introduced in the previous chapter had an expectation of where to find God. Problems developed when that expectation was not met. Confusion, anger, disappointment, or indifference resulted.

All persons agreed that if there is a God, then God must be somewhere. In addition, God must be doing something. Each of them in turn expected to find God protecting a loved one, creating in the deep recesses of the earth, presiding over the invisible courtroom of the universe, speaking within the depths of the human mind, or viewing our world from a distance as an artist reflects upon a finished work.

Sue's world was turned upside down by the accidental death of her steady boyfriend. Listening to her painful cry, we know that she expected God to be present in some way in Tom's accident. Neither Ron's God who is far away and uninvolved nor the minister's God who plucks people off the face of the earth to carry out some holy mission would do for Sue. God was to be present doing something.

Her conviction was that God protects and saves. Her God was one who does not allow the death of a young man just beginning to taste life. Her God was one of power who can step in and make things happen.

Although unclear exactly how God might prevent the accident, Sue expected that there was some way to do so. If God knows everything and can do anything, then surely there was a way. But there was an even more puzzling part of the tragedy for Sue. God could have saved Tom. God did not. Why? What was the reason? Sue could not fit two things together: God loves and protects people and God allows the accident.

Sue was looking for God in loving protection. God was not found there.

Walt and Marian had lived many years longer than Sue. They had been seasoned by unfair situations, unanswered questions, and untimely deaths. They would not share the same indignation and despair as a teenager in her first collision with tragedy.

They did not expect that God would swoop down like Superman or Wonder Woman and cap the spewing volcano. Still, at this particular moment in their lives, they were overwhelmed by a horrendous natural disaster. They expected that God would reward them for years of hard work and sacrifice. They expected God to fulfill their lives, from seeds planted to fruits harvested.

This expectation was drastically violated, a contract broken. Walt and Marian were looking for God in the covenant of rich blessings returned for long faithfulness. They also found it hard to fit such violent destruction into how things work in nature. In this way they had a more

30

difficult task than Sue, for she did not think that God had any part in causing the accident. A volcanic eruption is different.

Was the answer to be found in the explanation that God played no part whatsoever in this eruption? There would be some relief in this answer, for no responsibility for the disaster would be placed upon God. However, if they embraced this answer, they would run headlong into another firmly held belief—God created the world and continues to create therein. An answer suggesting God's absence from God's own creation was hardly satisfying.

Starting from the opposite side, what if God did play some part in the eruption? Now they were left puzzling over God's purposes in such an event. That God might participate in acts that radically alter and destroy life was utterly mysterious to them.

Was some lesson to be taught? Could some greater good be gained that might justify the far-reaching destruction? What could be a benefit that was worth more than the life and beauty lost? Or was the lesson that God's ways are finally unknowable?

Walt and Marian looked for God in a covenant, just as laborers of old anticipated the vineyard owner's pay at the end of a hard day's work, but found no coins. They looked for God in the cause of the spewing smoke and ashes, but found only confusion!

Juan rings out clearly the expectation that God makes things right, fair, and just. While speaking from the idealism of childhood, he also stands in a long line of prophetic tradition.

Let justice roll down like waters, and righteousness like an ever-flowing stream (Amos 5:24).

What does the Lord require of you but to do justice, and to love kindness, and to walk humbly with your God? (Micah 6:8).

Many throughout the centuries would agree with Juan's stress on God's justice. No one needed to tell him that the massacre was grossly unfair. The God who is on the side of right should have stepped in and stopped it. In movies and television dramas, the forces of right arrive just in the nick of time to save the day. God was to act accordingly.

A young boy faces the classical problem of evil: if God is all-powerful and God is all-good, why is there evil in the world? Surely, an almighty and good God could stop evil, could have prevented evil from ever getting started, or, indeed, could make good things happen. The glaring evidence of unfairness, injustice, and inhumanity seen in all directions says that for some reason God is not doing any of these. Something is awry. There is a "fly in the ointment."

Juan, like Sue, was looking for God as the just and powerful one who could have prevented the wrong. He emerged from the carnage shaken.

Sarah shares more with Ron than the others, for she was not caught in any fiery moment. Her expectation of God was unmet in many moments over years of time, eroding her belief like small drops of water dripping on a rock. She had been looking for God within her own mind.

Sarah's search is not without precedent. In the late eighteenth century, Friedrich Schleiermacher focused the search for God in human experience. His own experience of absolute dependence upon God was the primary evidence he needed for belief in God.

Like her German predecessor, Sarah thought that God would be known in her sensations, feelings, thoughts, fantasies, ideas, brainstorms, and reflections. God should have stood out in some way in her ongoing stream of experience. God should have been visible rather than merely part of the landscape. God should have been heard rather than blending into the orchestra.

Sarah wanted to point to her inner experiences and say, "Yes, there is God. Right there!" Something distinctive was needed—a vision, a nudge, a call, a still small voice. Finding God to be hidden, she gave up the search. Sarah concluded that if there is a God, that same God had eluded her!

Ron had it the easiest of all the persons—no hurt, disappointment, or anger. He simply did not expect God to be present today. God's work is essentially done and God is now watching, resting, or doing other things in other places.

Although he would probably not recognize the name of William Paley, Ron was indebted to him for the belief that he now embraced. This eighteenth-century English thinker had created the image of the "Watchmaker" for the God who made and wound the watch.

Ron also stood on the shoulders of another famous English scientist, whose name he probably did know—Sir Isaac Newton. This genius discovered the universal laws by which all of Ron's marvelous machinery operates. Nearly three hundred years of scientific research since Newton stood behind Ron and his present beliefs about God.

Walking in the footsteps of Charles Darwin, a third well-known English thinker, Ron wondered at times if God had made and wound the great watch at all. Perhaps everything had simply evolved by chance and selection. If God were doing something now to make the awesome laws of nature work, Ron would be interested to know what that might be. He remained skeptical, however, as to what is needed beyond the explanations of biology, chemistry, and

33

physics. If at all, Ron looked for God back there or out there. For him God was truly out of this world!

Where have these persons been looking for God? All agreed, except Ron, that God is present in some way and involved in some manner. God is somewhere doing something. They agreed that God has power to make things happen and that God does not always exercise this power. How the power works and for what reasons the power is used or withheld remain unclear. All appealed to God as the source of justice and fairness, yet the puzzle centers on the widespread presence of injustice and unfairness.

Now it is possible to raise the questions that are central to this entire discussion. Have these persons been looking in the appropriate places for God? Could it be that the problem lies in the particular expectations they have held of God?

The task of this book is to address the questions raised by these persons and to offer a new image of God that more adequately answers them. If the persons portrayed here had held this image of God, they would have emerged more positively from their situations. New explanations would have been available in their confusing moments. New comfort would have been present in their painful moments.

The next chapter is the story of Tom's biking accident, the reason for Sue's grief. It is a close-up description of God's presence and participation in each stage of the developing accident. The story is the beginning of a new answer to Sue—and to Walt, Marian, Juan, Sarah, and Ron. An answer is given to the question: Where in Tom's world is God?

II.

FORMING AN ANSWER:

A Unique Presence in Every Moment

3.

God's Role in a Biking Accident

*T*OM sat in English class, his thoughts occasionally drifting away from the discussion. During one of these daydreams, the idea occurred to him to have lunch with Sue at the downtown drive-in. This idea emerged out of God's continuing persuasion that Tom experience enjoyment. The thought pleased Tom as he turned it over in his mind.

Between classes Tom found Sue at her locker and suggested the plan for lunch. She liked the idea. God was present with both Sue and Tom, feeling the anticipation with them as they planned together. Since Sue needed to stop by her house to pick up her pom-poms for drill team practice that afternoon, she would drive and meet Tom there.

The final class of the morning seemed to creep by for Tom in spite of God encouraging him toward the excitement of learning. Even a Caring Friend is ignored at times. Tom divided his attention between thinking about Sue and gazing out the window at the apple trees just then beginning to bud. The lunch bell jolted Tom from his reverie. He scooped up his books from the desk and ran out of the building. The Caring One felt the excitement with him.

Tom fitted the key into the ignition, opened the throttle, and with two firm thrusts of his foot started the cycle. He loved the surge of power when the engine roared. God felt the surge right along with Tom. Kicking up the stand, Tom turned the accelerator on the handle, held on the brakes, and "burned rubber" out of the parking lot.

It seemed to be the only place during his day where he had some freedom to be himself. All day he was told what to do. A term paper had to be written, Thursday's homework was due, Biology was a required class, holding hands was not allowed in the hallways, eight minutes was the time limit for changing classes.

Gently, as a Caring Friend, God called Tom toward pleasure in this day. He might drink in the emerging beauty, see the vivid colors, and feel the warmth of the spring sun. He could hear his mother exclaim that this is her favorite time of year. He also recalled Sue's excitement at seeing the first purple crocus peeking out from beneath a clump of brown leaves. In fact, Tom divided his attention between enjoying the present and looking forward to what was next. God was enjoying this experience with Tom, as well as relating to the birds singing on the branches, the newly formed buds on the apple trees, and the dog lying lazily in the sun.

Tom felt a mood of caution blending with his feelings of pleasure. The wind whipping through his hair prompted him to remember that he did not have his helmet on. He could picture it still in his locker.

The impulse toward caution rose more strongly from the Caring Friend. His father's stern lecture about always wearing a helmet came ringing clearly to his ears. He had

38

heard it so often he knew it by heart. His brother Art's merciless teasing that only sissies wear those "dumb-looking things" was his next thought.

For a fleeting moment Tom considered going back for his helmet, but he quickly shook the idea off. It was too much bother, and it would take away from his already short time with Sue. His real fear, however, was that Mr. Simpson might be waiting to talk about his noisy exit from the parking lot. Tom returned his attention to the free and easy feeling of a young man on his bike on a beautiful day. Although this was different than God had envisioned these next moments, the Loving Friend experienced the freedom also.

Tom had driven this road between school and town so many times that he could do it blindfolded. He knew the road by its feel—each bump, incline, pothole, curve, and straightaway. Each time he enjoyed the tingling feeling of leaning into the curve, a reminder of the rides at the carnival. The Caring Friend shared the tingling with Tom.

Nearing the curve, Tom felt again the urge to use care. The tension in his body told him that he had mixed feelings. Some impulses pulled him to let up on the hand throttle and touch the brakes. These feelings probably arose from the class he had taken on biking and Sue's "be careful" following each farewell. Others pulled toward loving the risk at hand. The chase scenes of the late movie flashed before his eyes. Tom moved ahead!

Seconds later Tom felt the bike begin to slide. The Caring Friend felt these sensations just as Tom did. Acting with computer-like speed, Tom let up on the gas, tightened his grip, and struggled to keep his balance. Yet all his rapid actions seemed to be of no avail. Tom was losing control fast. Tires no longer gripped the surface of the road.

The Loving Friend felt this loss of control in Tom's body

39

just as Tom did. Tom tightened every muscle. Adrenalin surged through his system. His heart pounded. Blood vessels in his arms and legs contracted.

Over the steep bank at the curve, machine and person were airborne. Loose gravel, flying sparks, and a cloud of dust marked the event. Consequences of earlier decisions were being carried out.

God felt with Tom the shudder of terror as he flew into the air. God experienced with Tom his desperate scream as he sighted the large tree directly in his pathway. A flow of utter helplessness streamed through Tom as he realized the impossibility of changing direction. No longer able to bear it, he tightly shut his eyes.

There was a violent crunch, followed by excruciating pain, star bursts, intense burning sensations, and fleeting visual memories. The Caring Friend suffered the shattering with Tom. Along with Tom, God felt a loss of feeling, then an overshadowing darkness. Tom died.

The police officer nervously rang the doorbell at the white frame house. God felt the officer's anxiety and shortness of breath. The woman was humming as she left the dining table and walked toward the door. The Caring Friend was present also with her. God will continue to be present as she feels her world turn upside down by learning that her son had just died.

Where was God in Tom's world? God was fully present and actively involved in every split-second of the developing accident. In each forming decision, God was persuading, encouraging, luring, and urging toward enjoyment, safety, and well-being. God knew Tom as the final decision-maker at every critical choice. God valued Tom's freedom to accept, reject, or shape any persuasion. God experienced every

40

nuance of feeling exactly as Tom did. God was neither totally absent from the tragic moments nor absolutely controlling them. Rather God was present in loving persuasion.

All this is an answer to Sue's burning questions. The answer differs from that of her expectations. She understood the almighty power of God as being able to make things happen exactly as God wills them to happen rather than as a Caring Friend's loving persuasion. God desired and longed for Tom's safety and well-being, but God also acknowledged and valued Tom's freedom. God is loving persuader rather than almighty controller.

If Sue had understood God in this way, her anguish could have been tempered by comfort. She could have fully mourned the loss of Tom, knowing that her Caring Friend and Fellow Sufferer was mourning with her. She could have avoided the struggle between believing that God could have saved Tom and wondering why God didn't save him.

Now we have before us a brief description of the accident and the interpretation it offers of where God is and what God does. The answer offered so far to the central question is that God is lovingly and persuasively present in each tiny event of life.

Next we turn to the source of this answer, the way in which God was present in the life of Jesus.

4.

The One Whom Jesus Called "Dadda"

GOD as a Caring Friend blossoms first and most fully in Jesus. It is from the significant moments in his life that this image of God is drawn. Now we turn to these moments to show where Tom's God is grounded.

Actually, Caring Friend is not strong enough. Jesus addressed God with the Aramaic word *Abba*, which is best translated "Daddy" or "Dadda." The intimacy implied is dramatically closer than Friend. We begin, then, with an intimate relationship.

To see how far this departs from the God known by many in the time of Jesus, we need to look at that world. In the tradition prior to Jesus, we find a variety of images of God. In all these images, God was involved in relationships. God was not standoffish. In those relationships, God at times appears to make things happen, while at other times God seems to persuade.

Indeed, God could make things happen! God created earth and humans (Gen. 1:1ff.), sent a massive flood (Gen. 6:17), turned people into pillars of salt (Gen. 19:26), made the sun stand still (Josh. 10:12), and parted the sea waters (Exod. 14:21).

In another mode, God bargained with Abraham about the destruction of a city (Gen. 18:23ff.), argued with the reluctant Moses (Exod. 3:7ff.), entered into a covenant with a people (Exod. 20:1ff.), and loved Israel like a child (Hosea 11:1ff.). A mixed picture of God's presence emerges.

The titles of this era—Creator, Lord, Judge, and King—stress power to make things happen even though God may choose to limit that power. Such images are in sharp contrast to the persuasion of a Loving Parent or a Caring Friend. Even the most benevolent King does not use persuasion as his primary method of reigning over a people: Creators create, Lords rule, Judges decide, and Kings proclaim.

In the time of Jesus one prevalent image of God was that of Lawgiver who is now in the far distant past. Not only the Ten Commandments but also a host of other minor laws had been designed to cover every conceivable situation. God related only to Israel, the covenant people, not to all humanity. This vision of lawgiver could hardly be consistent with persuasion.

Into this mixed scene Jesus entered addressing God in the most familiar form: Loving Parent. Hosea's beautiful image of God whose arms gathered up Israel and who taught Ephraim to walk is now center stage (Hosea 11:1ff.). Jesus' tone in addressing God and in teaching style was a new and radical departure from tradition. Jesus taught with authority, using the phrase, "I say to you," in contrast to the more common phrase, "It is written." The Gospels are replete with the astonished response, "for he taught them as one who had authority" (Matt. 7:29).

When Jesus used "I," his contemporaries were impressed with his authority, yet we today may see it as an expression of his freedom. Jesus spoke as though he were the one deciding what to say. There is no sense of being forced to speak as a child who might say, "My mother says that I have to . . . ." Nor did Jesus sound like a spokesman for some greater authority like the prophetic "Thus says the Lord." Jesus' manner of speaking is yet another clue to a persuasive relationship with a Caring Friend.

Prayer for Jesus was not to be modelled after the lengthy Gentile or the status-seeking Jewish prayers (Matt. 6:5, 7). Rather, prayer was to be a short utterance which begins by addressing the Father (Matt. 6:9). Jesus' prayer implied a closeness in which God already knew what was needed by the one in prayer. To teach such an understanding of prayer, Jesus must have felt himself intimately known by God.

In contrast to the Law, Jesus used a new phrase, "the kingdom of God" (Matt. 12:28; Mark 4:26; Luke 10:9). He affirmed the Law, yet transformed it. "You have heard . . . of old . . . but I say to you . . . " (Matt. 5:21ff.). He also proclaimed, "You shall love the Lord your God" (Matt. 22:37). He told those gathered that the sabbath was made for persons, not persons for the sabbath (Mark 2:27). Boldness prevailed! Transformation abounded!

Jesus' most striking actions, as well as those most dangerous to his personal safety, were violations of the law. He healed on the sabbath (Luke 13:10ff.), touched unclean lepers (Mark 1:41), talked with Gentile women (John 4:7), forgave an adulteress (John 8:3ff.), and associated with tax collectors (Matt. 9:10ff.). Worst of all, he ate with sinners (Luke 5:29ff.). If these violations were not bad enough, Jesus claimed that the actions simply reflected the desires of God. His contemporaries were justifiably enraged by such brashness.

While all this shows the newness which Jesus brought to old situations, it also illustrates the theme of God's love for

45

all persons. The Law was often read as if it left sinners outside of God's care, but the realm of God proclaimed by Jesus included them. Sinners were ill and in need of a physician, lost and in need of a shepherd. In all the love expressed, Jesus appeared to speak and act freely, not as one compelled or forced.

Although the parable was not a new form, the content with which Jesus filled that form was new. These surprising, even shocking stories served to reveal the activity of God. By both tradition and custom the father of the prodigal was to consider his son dead for radically violating his own faith in a distant land (Luke 15:11ff.). However, he responded in a dramatically new and forgiving way.

The parent ran to meet the youth—an infrequent occurrence for an elderly Middle Eastern landowner. He embraced and kissed his son—a well-known symbol of pardon; draped a robe on his shoulders—an honor reserved for a visiting dignitary; placed a ring—a sign of authority—on his finger; brought sandals for his feet—the distinction of a free person from a slave; and ordered the fatted calf to be slaughtered and a feast to begin—a rare meal and celebration in that era. Each new act by the parent must have added to the shock of the listener of Jesus' time.

Jesus' story leaves little doubt as to the activity of God. The new floods into an old situation. Jesus tells of overflowing love for the undeserving one. We may wonder if Jesus could have created this story without first experiencing himself such love from the Persuasive Presence. The story serves as a clue to the experience of the storyteller.

The now familiar Good Samaritan was an equally shocking story to the original listeners (Luke 10:25ff.). Of those who would be expected to aid the wounded person, only the despised foreigner does so. Moreover, the aid is abundant. The foreigner places the man on an ass, takes him

46

to an inn, and tells the innkeeper that all expenses will be paid.

Like the story of the prodigal, this story illustrates a surprising, unbounded love. The listener cannot miss the point. What is more, the storyteller claims that this is what God's activity is like. Again, we may wonder to what degree this created story reflects Jesus' experience with God.

The parable of the vineyard owner is likewise intriguing (Matt. 20:1ff.). The owner pays the laborers the exact amount he had contracted with them for a day's work. Out of generosity he chooses to pay the same amount to others who worked only an hour. While some rejoice and others grumble, the owner asserts his right to be generous.

Again, Jesus creates a story about a person who acts in a new way in an old situation. Undeserved caring is offered. Again, the story is told to illustrate God's realm. Once again, the puzzle is where Jesus would find the makings for such stories when the culture in which he lived did not provide them. Perhaps the answer is in his own continuing relationship with the Caring One.

Our picture of how God was present with Jesus now takes us to the last week of Jesus' life, commonly called the passion narrative. That which is most instructive about Jesus' relationship with God is what did not happen. Jesus did not raise an army, even after the rejoicing crowds swarmed around his triumphal entry into Jerusalem. Surely this was disappointing to many, especially to the Zealots, who were convinced that the Messiah would forcibly overthrow Roman authority.

Following his arrest, Jesus did not deny his actions. He did not recant his teaching in hopes of securing his personal freedom. Nor was there a dramatic "James Bond" type escape from the prison or violent response to the insults and brutal lashings of the soldiers. In the excruciating moments of agony following crucifixion, Jesus forgave those who had just carried out the deed (Luke 23:34). He did not respond to those who taunted that while he saved others he could not save himself (Mark 15:31).

Throughout his agonizing, Jesus did not exert miraculous, almighty, or coercive power. Nor is there evidence that Jesus was required to endure such an ending. Rather, it appears that Jesus was making choices freely in each labored step from the garden to the cross.

In reviewing these features of the life of Jesus, there appears to be an emerging theme in his teaching and actions. People are radically changed into persons who are surprisingly different than the culture around them. Persons who would be expected to judge harshly or to rigorously follow the Law offer undeserved and overflowing love. It appears impossible that this theme could have emerged if Jesus himself were experiencing a legalistic, coercive, or distant relationship with God.

A more likely explanation is that Jesus knew a lovingly persuasive God, who served as the wellspring of all Jesus' words and acts. His way of speaking to God was as a little child to a loving parent. Out of that rich relationship grew a new way of teaching, a new form of prayer, a new style of story, a wider relationship with varied people, and a new acceptance of suffering and death. The Gospel writer John expressed the words of Jesus well: "As the Father has loved me, so have I loved you; abide in my love" (John 15:9). Tom's God is grounded here!

Although the focus has been upon the relationship of Jesus with God as Caring Friend, that was not the only relationship in which Jesus engaged. Rather, God was present as one central relationship in the midst of other relationships. It is this web of relationships of Jesus which we now examine to see more fully how the Caring Friend and Persuasive Presence was active in each unfolding event in Jesus' life.

Jesus was influenced by relationships with his body, his personal past, the world's past, and the present situation, in addition to God. Each of these relationships needs to be illustrated.

Jesus was related to his body. He walked the dusty roadways, ate bread, drank wine, grew weary, slept, and agonized. Likewise, Jesus was related to a personal past in which he was the decider and the actor. His past included a birthplace, brothers and sisters, a hometown, a circumcision ceremony, pilgrimages to Jerusalem, and a vocation of carpentry. As an adult he made decisions as he encountered Pharisees, tax collectors, prostitutes, soldiers, children, lepers, Gentiles, and Roman authorities.

Like everyone else in his day, Jesus was related to the world's past. He was immersed in the tradition of Israel and affected by its great institutions of patriarch, king, priest, prophet, synagogue, and Torah. He was impacted by Roman rule. He knew the local folklore and spoke Aramaic, a language similar to Hebrew. These great forces influenced Jesus.

As with everyone else, one situation unfolded into another in his life. Jesus was related to each present situation. So many were already defined by the Law. Jesus knew the expectations of given situations: one stands to read the Law and Prophets and sits to teach; one does not heal on the sabbath; and one uses unleavened bread in the Passover feast to remember the hurried escape from Egypt.

For Jesus all these relationships were similar to every human of his time and place. In the midst of this web of relationships the Caring Friend spoke. In this web the Persuading Presence was active as one of the relationships which made up each moment of Jesus' life.

This activity of the Caring Friend can be seen in such a moment as Jesus' encounter with Zacchaeus (Luke 19:2ff.). We turn now to that encounter. Jesus' body must have cried out "danger" as he moved toward the tree where the small-framed tax collector had climbed. Anyone's body places survival for itself first. No one could violate religious law, such as that against eating with sinners, without feeling the pangs of anxiety and tension about penalties. Indeed, the crowd might have turned quickly against him in the next moment for breaking the law.

Jesus must have remembered stories he had heard about the traitorous tax collectors and their abuse of his people. As a child he must have watched wide-eyed as his family paid the hated and burdensome taxes. In contrast, his more recent past must have included a number of events in which he had already expressed God's love for unattractive persons. Mixed feelings, images, and pictures would come forth from his past.

Jesus knew the world around him. He knew of this man's utter disregard for God. He knew of the law under which they both lived. The law was clear: Israelites do not eat with sinners.

Mixed impulses must have tugged and pulled. Walk on by! Ignore him! Keep your distance from the despicable! Engage the unattractive one with love! Thus spoke the web of relationships.

In the midst of this blend of relationships was Jesus' central relationship to God, persuading him to encounter the person in a radically new and loving way. To engage Zaccheus in love or to follow the law was the choice. Either could have been the decision. Jesus chose once again the vision of God! "Zacchaeus . . . I must stay at your house today" (Luke 19:5).

This scene would be repeated time and again: reaching

out to touch a leper, speaking with the Gentile woman, and forgiving an adultress. All were acts filled with danger; all were radical departures from tradition. All show the wondrous persuasion of a gracious God. All reflect the Caring Friend as one unique relationship among many relationships.

The image of Caring Friend grows out of the experiences of Jesus. The Persuading Presence speaks in the midst of other voices. In these experiences Jesus adventured in dramatically new acts of boundless love and gave to all the future a new image of God.

It is this theme which will now be expanded more fully in the next chapter. Having located the Caring Friend in the web of Jesus' relationships, we now turn to how this One is centrally present in all human lives.

5.

How God Is Present with All People

WE experience ourselves as one; we experience ourselves as many. Both are true. In the dramatic extremes we know of Dr. Jekyll and Mr. Hyde, the three faces of Eve, and Sybil. In scripture we hear the man lament to Jesus "My name is Legion; for we are many" (Mark 5:9).

In our daily experience we feel the many and the one. We push a tray past the desserts in the cafeteria line. We come home to find a sick child just as we were ready to pack the last suitcase for a couple's weekend away. Many voices speak! It is easier to accept that we may be different from time to time than to know that we are many in a single moment.

The problem becomes one of how to talk about this condition. Many answers are available today, some decrying this state of being, others rejoicing in its complexity. The answer offered here is that each human event is like a council meeting, and in each such council meeting God as Caring Friend is present. It is this image of council meeting which will serve as the heart of the matter throughout the remainder of this and following chapters; therefore, it is worthy of a pause to describe clearly the image.

In a council meeting, while there are many present, there is one meeting. There are many voices, yet one conclusion. There is complexity, there is blending. It is important at this point to describe in more detail a council meeting. The description is similar to Tom rounding a curve or Jesus encountering Zacchaeus. The idea covers both.

The chairs are set in a circle, the coffeepot perks nearby, and the blackboard has been wiped clean. Council members arrive, greeting each other, then moving gradually to their chairs. Each member considers the minutes of the previous meeting, and the chairperson for this meeting asks for the approval of the minutes.

The agenda for this evening's meeting is presented and written on the blackboard. Something is up, otherwise there would be no need to call a meeting. Luckily for the group today it is a problem which should be relatively easy to solve.

Various council members speak out, for each represents the interests of a separate group of people. Questions are raised to clarify the decision at hand. Solutions are proposed. Some disagree with certain suggestions. Feelings are expressed.

An older member reminds the council how a similar problem was solved in the past. Others listen but want to approach the problem in a new way. The group becomes divided. One member proposes a plan to combine the best of both ideas. The feeling tone changes from tension to relief.

After making some minor changes in the compromise solution, one council member moves its adoption. Another seconds. Two members who are not totally happy with the compromise attempt to amend the motion. Their attempt fails. The question is called and the motion carries. The decision is made and the meeting is adjourned.

As members visit after the meeting, several are surprised that the final answer was one that no member was promoting before they began. Ideas had been proposed, rejected, revised, and shaped during the flow of the meeting. Nothing ended up quite the way it started. Each council member had opportunity to shape the final answer. Not all spoke nor were all totally satisfied, but they accepted the solution.

There are many types of council meetings, as there are many types of human events. Some are harmonious agreement, friendly compromise, tense stand-off, utter standstill, business as usual, rubber stamp, divided house, yelling match, or mob scene. Again, like human events, they can be tremendously enjoyable, utterly boring, or intensely painful. Tom's experiences of free and easy riding followed instantly by an agonizing accident show such variety.

We have seen what a council meeting does. There is a process with a beginning, an ending, and stages in between. A human event is like that too—a very tiny meeting in which something is accomplished.

Having looked at what it does, now we may consider who makes up the council meeting of a human event. Obviously, they are council members. Many are present. All are facets of the same one person. While in the earlier example each council member represented a group of people, in a human event the council members represent relationships. We saw this web of relationships in our presentation of Jesus earlier.

One council member is a relationship to one's own body, a second council member is a relationship to one's past, a third is a relationship to the world's past, a fourth is a relationship to the immediate situation, and the final and most central council member is a relationship to God. Relationships are what make up an event. The council meeting becomes a shorthand way of saying that all human events are filled with a rich variety of relationships.

So it can be summarized that a human event is composed of relationships and that each event creates something from those relationships. There is content; there is process. Each human event has both. Every human event has at least five such council members. Each one is a vital relationship. Each relationship is one of many involved simultaneously in any event. Now, each council member needs to be introduced.

The first council member is our relationship to our body. Through this council member we receive the vast sensory information of seeing, hearing, touching, smelling, and tasting. Many of our most satisfying experiences occur in this relationship—seeing Mount Rainier from the air, hearing a meadowlark, kissing a lover, diving into Lake Chelan, smelling a rose, savoring the first ear of summer corn, breathing in the crisp, cool air of a fall morning.

This council member places items on the agenda frequently and exerts great influence in every meeting. Its aim is to bring about pleasurable sensual experiences. On the other hand, this same member can radically disrupt any meeting by a throbbing toothache, a pounding headache, or a piercing chest pain.

Never absent, this council member both enriches and shatters human events. Only the radical acts of amputation, paralysis, or unconsciousness may limit the relationship. Only the moment of death severs the relationship.

A second council member is our relationship to our personal past. Usually we call this relationship "memory." In any new event we can recall earlier events like it, including what we felt, thought, and did. How we did something in the past is one of the most influential voices in any council meeting as to how to do it now.

Also, the people who were a part of our past loom large in the present. The powerful words and feelings expressed by parents, brothers, sisters, relatives, and friends have shaping influence. Our own decisions about who we are, made in response to those persons, are frequently the loudest voice in any council meeting.

It is so easy to take for granted the fact that we remember who we have been. Only the opposite extreme brings out its importance. Even temporary amnesia is traumatic! As we awaken to each new dawning, we do not have to learn anew to walk, talk, or write. The Lord's Prayer or the pledge of allegiance to the flag comes forth when requested. All this is due to this council member. The far-reaching influence of this member is partly due to the ease of repeating the familiar rather than struggling with the unknown. Both helpful guide and self-imprisoning guard, this council member is ever present.

The relationships to our body and our personal past are crucial, but we are also related to an environment. We do not live in a vacuum. Thus, the third council member is our relationship to the past events of the world. "Past" can mean not only years, centuries, or eons, but also the state of the world a second ago. This council member represents the entire history of the biosphere, inorganic entities, plants, animals, and humans. The past of the world is filled with events where we were not present and over which we had no control.

People again loom large. Those of earlier generations whom we read about or hear about but never knew ourselves still shape us. The heroes and heroines, the martyrs and explorers, the exploiters and cowards, the successes and the failures serve as guides for us to emulate or avoid. Groups formed long ago to further some cause lure us or even demand that we order our lives around their cherished values.

Our relationship is most specifically and intensely to the adventures which have occurred on planet Earth. Every council meeting is greatly affected by the presence of gravity, the quality of air, the food and water supply, the urban sprawl, the inherited forms of family, and the threat of nuclear holocaust. This council member is our relationship to our ever-changing surroundings.

The fourth council member represents our relationship to the immediate situation. This member relates to all that is immediately present to our awareness. The variety of situations in which we place ourselves is endless—standing before the marriage altar, boarding a jet for Hawaii, running out of gas on a busy Los Angeles freeway, hearing the sound of footsteps from behind while walking alone at night, waiting for the physician to report the results of an exploratory biopsy, or hearing the last class bell ring before Christmas vacation.

If there is anything we can count on, it is that situations change. This member of the council keeps us up to date on this change. While the present situation will dissolve quickly into our own past and the world's past, for a short duration it is the present to us. It is where the action is. Coping with this situation is the reason a council meeting is held.

The fifth and final council member represents our relationship to God. Once having all the known facts about our body, our past, the world's past, and the present situation, this relationship centers upon a slightly different area—who we might become. This is the arena of potential. Through this member the council meeting is offered possibilities for how to face a given situation. The member presents a vision which, if accepted, would begin to transform who we have been.

This council member is unique and speaks as a unique voice in any meeting, for the focus is upon what could be rather than what already exists. The relationship always offers a lure to go beyond who we have been before. This lure takes into account who one has been and who one is now, but is not limited to that.

God as the Caring Friend is the bringer of these possibilities. We are usually aware only of the possibility and not the Bringer, the actions of the Persuasive Presence and not the Presence.

Each possibility is offered from a vast reservoir within God's life and is always characterized by love. Each emerges after God first experiences with us our feelings of the previous moment. The lure is given for the next moment only after knowing us intimately from within. This relationship is one of sympathetic understanding.

Following each council meeting God saves that event in God's own life. However small or insignificant, each is taken into God's own being forever. The results of every council meeting are saved. This relationship is one of endless cherishing.

As has already been emphasized, this council member represents a persuasive voice. Although possibilities are offered for each meeting, there is no guarantee that the council meeting will accept them. Nor is there any requirement that it do so. Quite the contrary, many lures are ignored, rejected, or radically modified in the process of the meeting. Since God's being is love, whether any lure is ignored or accepted, God will feel the results, save them, and offer a new vision for the next meeting.

So the five council members have gathered. They represent relationships to body, personal past, world's past, immediate situation, and God. There may be five or fifty. All are in place. Now let us allow them to come alive in the unfolding of Tom's accident.

Tom had a series of council meetings in which all

council members participated. Changing relationships with his body played a major part. He saw the beauty of spring about him and felt the wind whipping through his hair. Because of his desire for the tingling sensation of rounding the curve, he did not slow down. His sense of balance gave him the first warnings of the imminent danger ahead. The violent impact left this relationship so damaged that Tom could no longer respond to persuasions from the Caring Friend.

Tom's past was highly active in the entire series of events. He did remember where the cycle was parked and how to start it. Each mile of the roadway was indelibly marked in his memory. Recalling the thrill of the curve was a primary persuader in his decision to move ahead rather than slow down.

Had he lived one hundred fifty years earlier in the same location, none of this could have occurred. The world's past was also a crucial member of each of Tom's council meetings. Asphalt highways, motorcycles, fast-food restaurants, and regional high schools are all past accomplishments which had been gifted to him. The combination of achievements necessary to fabricate a motorcycle is staggering. All had to be in place for the drama to occur.

Situations change rapidly for a fast-moving biker. The relationship to the immediate situation represents a vital council member to Tom. Moving along with total ease changes in a split second to life-threatening danger. Once sliding on the curve, Tom was there. He could not go back to the safe situation of seconds ago. All that he was relating to seconds ago became totally outdated. Full-scale emergency meetings were now the order of the day for the council.

As the final council member, God was actively offering options in each new unfolding event. Each lure was toward enjoyment, safety, and life. Some were accepted, others rejected. Like the rapidly changing situation, possibilities of a moment ago were utterly outdated by Tom's most recent choice. Radically adjusted possibilities became necessary—how to stay alive rather than how to enjoy rounding the curve!

Obviously, different relationships assumed greater importance in each succeeding event. Tom's past, sounding a call to repeat an exciting sensation, was dominant in those events. God felt each event with Tom before giving the next new possibility. Cherishing that moment forever followed whatever Tom did with that possibility.

The five council members have been introduced and their contributions to Tom's accident illustrated. In the mix of these relationships, the drama of human life unfolds. Of course, there may be many council members depending upon the particular meeting. It must be at least a quintet, but it could easily enlarge into a Boston Symphony Orchestra. The influence of each member will wax and wane, never remaining the same during a meeting or from one meeting to the next. If meetings were colors, they would look like a rotating kaleidoscope. No council member is ever the permanent chairperson. Rather, in the fluxing council meeting different members may rise to be the leader at any time. Leadership shifts rapidly.

Human events are like council meetings, each with a beginning and an ending, flowing one after another. Past meetings deeply affect but do not control the becoming one. The Caring Voice of new possibilities is always present. There is a blending and mixing of voices which leads to the coming together at the end. Which voices will emerge as most persuasive is difficult to predict. We can only know that many voices will always be present.

Each council meeting has only one agenda item. The meeting is called, a solution reached, and the council adjourns. A new meeting is called a moment later to grapple with the next agenda. In this way there is continuity and there is change. Since one council member is always related to what has been, there is a guarantee of continuity. Since another is always related to what might be, there is at least the hope for change.

So then, where in the world is God? God is actively present in each tiny human event persuading us by loving visions to transform ourselves continually. God is one of our constant relationships. God is in the midst of our deepest processes. Like one unique voice in a choir, one special instrument in an orchestra that blends with the many others, God is present persuading the many to become one in beauteous harmony.

6.

Opening Ourselves to God's Presence

HOW, then, do we open ourselves to the Caring Friend, who is ever present in our council meetings? How do we listen for God's unique voice in the midst of a multitude of voices? How do we form a relationship with God?

It is to these questions which we now turn, for they are the finally important ones. The first step in answering will be to compare three pictures of God's presence in the world. Comparing allows us to see that differences in thinking about God and imaging of God lead us to quite different spiritual practices. This comparison will prepare us to view the practices which grow out of the image of the Caring Friend.

Three live options of picturing God are as Watchmaker, as Judge, and as Caring Friend. While they surely do not represent all the options, they do portray vivid differences. If we think of the world as one great machine and God as the one who created that machine, then an image that expresses that idea is the Watchmaker. God produced the watch, wound it, and is now at some distance observing the watch run on its own.

This thinking and imaging would lead us naturally to certain practices. The most basic would be to follow the laws by which the machine runs. Not to do so would lead to disaster. We might admire and worship God for such a wondrous creation, but we would not expect to find God in our hours and days. God would be above it all, high and lifted up.

It follows that we would need to develop our own standards and morals for everyday living. The content of our prayer would be adoration, praise, and gratefulness or mediation in which we would have only ourselves as listener.

Decisions would be made by finding out how the world works and fitting in with it. Any decision would be purely and simply our own choice without any influence from God. There would be little room for a close relationship with God, for at best it would be like admiring the artist who painted the beautiful picture we are now beholding.

If, however, we think of God as the creator and sustainer of justice, then the image of the Judge in the Great Courtroom appears naturally. While the Watchmaker is an image of the scientific era, the Judge is one of the earlier biblical and medieval images.

Relating to God would come through the sacred laws. Our ultimate concern to know those laws would lead us to continual and exhaustive study. We would burn the midnight oil, pouring over the books. We would pray for understanding of any statute which was not entirely clear. We would center upon walking the straight and narrow path in accordance with the law.

Our thoughts about ourselves and others would focus upon right and wrong, good and bad, obedience and rebellion. We would be eager to find ways to be forgiven if we violated the law knowingly out of rebellion or unknowingly out of ignorance. A major fear would be whether or not we would be found acceptable at the time of the judgment at the close of our lives. The practice of those living in the shadow of the Judge would be quite different from those living as a cog in the great Watch. In either case, practice grows out of thinking and imaging.

In contrast to these two images stands the picture of the Caring Friend. This picture grows out of the concept of God as the loving persuader in the world. The first basic difference is that the Caring Friend is a dear friend to all of life. God's relationship to the world is neither as Watchmaker winding the watch nor as Judge presiding over the courtroom, but as Caring Friend embracing life.

The world is not a lifeless machine running by eternal laws or a mere courtroom in which the human drama is played out; rather it is a web of billions upon billions of living events. The world is composed of innumerable events, each one creating its own new adventures. Like the human events which have been described here, all life is made up of council meetings. In each, the past pushes, God's possibilities pull, and action results. Animals, birds, and plants hold their own unique forms of council meetings. Moreover, we are interwoven with life; we are members of their council meetings and they members of ours.

Most often we do not recognize the tiny new events occurring in nature, since the changes from one council meeting to the next are so exceedingly small. In fact, it is their very routineness which provides us a world we can count on. But when we look closely, change is clearly visible.

In this image, God persuades life, just as God persuades us. The Caring Friend lures all creation. The Caring Friend is a part of *every* council meeting *everywhere!*

With this understanding of God and world we see ourselves in a new light, both who we are and those with

65

whom we live. We are part of the whole creation which is being called by loving persuasion. We are intertwined in a global web, a wondrous network.

This world is not divided into spirit and matter, sacred and secular, holy and mundane. All life is a continuing series of events. All are busily engaged in creating themselves from the divine call to be more beautiful and harmonious. Nor is the world divided into subjects, namely ourselves, and objects, namely animals, birds, and trees. All are beings which are to be addressed as I-Thou, rather than things to be used, controlled, or manipulated.

Sages, poets, and saints have glimpsed this vision. We are moved with Albert Schweitzer to hold a reverence for life. We gaze upon a statue of St. Francis and see the ever-present bird on his shoulder or in his hand. With Moses we hear the voice from the burning bush, "Put off your shoes from your feet, for the place on which you are standing is holy ground" (Exod. 3:5). With Maria we sing, "The hills are alive with the sound of music." So, God as Caring Friend invites us to love all whom God loves, to feel all life as embraced by the sacred.

Now we turn to the unique spiritual practices which emerge from this thinking and imaging. We begin simply by talking to ourselves differently. In our affirmations we will remind ourselves that the Caring Friend is present in each split second of our daily lives. It is so easy for us to slip into the notion that God is up there or out there involved with the really important matters somewhere else in the universe. We need to remind ourselves constantly that God is wondrously able to relate to "all creatures great and small" and that we are dearly beloved to God. We will keep whispering to ourselves that God loves the world. That which John Wesley affirmed can help: "Best of all, God is with us"!

Following from the way we talk to ourselves, our central

spiritual practice is increasing our awareness of God's persuasion. We may variously interpret this as watching for, listening for, or feeling for the possibilities which are always an offering to us. Some of us are more attuned to one channel than another. "I hear what you are saying," "I see what you mean," and "I just feel it's right" reflect these pathways.

Discovering which of these channels is the most natural for each of us is, consequently, an important step in developing spiritually. To respect and encourage others as they use a different channel is another important step, for therein we can enrich one another. In our great diversity as humans, it is most exciting that some feel God's nudge, others see God's vision, and still others hear that still small voice. While we have a usual channel, we may also open ourselves to other channels within us.

By whichever pathway the persuasion comes, it is a form of direction. This direction answers the question, Who shall I be next? It is heartening to know that since we all experience some sense of what to do next, spirituality is a natural process for all rather than a gift to the saintly few. Such nudgings as "I just feel that I need to clear the air with her" or "Getting that letter written just keeps nagging at me" are ordinary experiences.

One difficulty with this direction is that it seems so ordinary and mundane, yet this is what is central to the entire vision of the Caring Friend. The direction given at the major crossroads of life is more obvious to us and is also fully acknowledged as God's luring.

Direction may come merely as a simple idea, like the light bulb turning on above the cartoon character in the comics, but more often new possibilities are complex and filled with feeling. Climbing the walls out of utter boredom may be as much a direction as the exciting challenge which keeps nipping at our heels like a puppy. A recurring headache or a stomach tied in knots may be signs of discontent announcing the call to new adventure. Possibilities may be gut-wrenching experiences and are surely not always greeted with open arms.

In quite another mood, directions may be the joyous aha! or wow! experience of finally reaching some new answer or insight. The coming together of earlier conflicting plans may be the persuasive lure for that moment.

Strangely enough, those aspects of us which we dislike the most can be the source of the Caring Friend's direction. Frequently we want to put to sleep, cut out, or get rid of those very parts of us which may be presenting the lure to become more beautiful and harmonious persons. Those feelings and thoughts which at first glance appear to be the alien and enemy may very well end up being a friendly messenger. The call is neither always pleasant nor always safe; consequently, aliens in our personal experience need to be explored carefully. Delving into the mysterious and puzzling dreams which fill our nights is another entry into the deeper recesses where God speaks a language of symbol and meaning.

But not all direction we experience is of God! We are painfully aware of the many pulls and tugs which have come from other council members besides God. Discerning which possibilities are more likely to be from God becomes another important spiritual discipline.

Although difficult, there are ways. After receiving a new sense of direction, we may evaluate it by looking back, looking around, and looking forward. Turning back, we search that which the past says about this potential direction. Like the fiddler standing precariously on the roof, we keep our balance by tradition. How does it accord with scripture, the words of Jesus, the historic church councils, and the acts of the saints and martyrs? Any considered act which does not capture the spirit of the community of the faithful is to be questioned.

As we look around, our first consideration is our own council. Will the new direction enhance or harm any of our important relationships? How will the act affect the human community and the wider global community with which we are intertwined? Will this act promote cooperation and harmony in the world?

Our looking around also includes considering what we know of God. Does the direction reflect the grace, love, and persuasion of God? Any act which is violent, coercive, or physically harmful to ourselves or any part of creation is suspect.

Looking ahead is the more difficult task, one which requires imagination. We first imagine the way we and the world might look in two days, six months, or ten years. Then we can wonder whether that future person or world will thank us for acting this way today. The harmed person of the future may respond with a loud No! The enhanced person might shout a resounding Yes! The question remains, Will we be glad in six months that we did it?

Besides looking, we may reflect upon how long this direction has been coming to us. It may be as fresh as the morning dew or as familiar as an old shoe. Neither should be discounted, but that which will not let us go or which greets us at every corner we turn deserves careful attention. Not only how long, but how powerfully the direction has been gripping us is another guideline. An interesting academic thought has nowhere near the potency of a heart's desire which we can see, hear, feel, and taste.

After looking carefully and reflecting, it is always helpful to rehearse. The new direction may be tried out in fantasy without costing us a penny. Rehearsals may be held without

69

any commitment yet to "put the show on the road." Acting out the direction in our mind's eye gives us a greater feel for the consequences both for us and for others.

A final note is important about direction. From what has been said, it would be easy to gain the impression that God's possibilities are always aimed at calling us into some new adventure, exciting challenge, or difficult task. While this is often true, the Caring Friend also calls us to rest and restore ourselves. In many of our harried times, the most important prompting may be to turn from the hot and dusty trail and sit in the shade of a tree by a cooling stream. Come, be refreshed! Let us be aware of the Comforter bringing us refreshing comfort.

We may rightly conclude that it is not always easy to discern the lure of the Caring Friend. It does come clothed in the language of the other members of our council. Most frequently, possibilities are not in the form of pure and pristine directions. At times, nonetheless, many have heard with just that clarity. The trumpet has sounded a clear note in the midst of the clamor of their lives. For those moments we are grateful, but we do not expect that to be the usual.

Then there is peace. It is that sense of peace which comes when we tell a trusted friend about our honest and sometimes unattractive feelings and still feel understood and valued. A healing occurs in that encounter. So it can be with God as the Caring Friend who understands us fully from within. So, likewise, it can be when we feel the deep satisfaction of completing some important but difficult adventure in our lives. To be aware of these moments of peace and to name them the presence of God is an important aspect of our spiritual practice.

It is as though God is embracing us while at the same time offering us the next opportunity for growth. To be aware only of new direction is to miss the understanding, empathic, loving relationship in which it is given. We are accepted; we are called to grow. More often we seem to be painfully aware of our lacking and inadequacy rather than of our peace, thus, removing ourselves from the Graceful One who holds us.

We may rather consider the image of the Caring Friend as grace and feel this grace enfolding us—even when we have failed and when we do not accept ourselves. This may be one of our most difficult disciplines! Paul Tillich named our task, "Accept that you are accepted."

And there is meaning. Meaning is the opposite of these words we too often hear today: "Who cares?" "What difference does it make?" "In a hundred years it won't matter anyway!" In this day when loss of meaning is so prevalent, we want our thoughts, words, and deeds to matter, to add up to something, to be important to someone. They matter to God.

Since the Caring Friend is so intimately close, God knows our every thought and participates in the struggle of every feeling to become a word. We are known. Even more, the Caring Friend saves each tiny event in God's own life everlastingly. Every small candle we light in the midst of darkness and every cup of cool water that we offer are cherished without end.

So we can celebrate that no matter how small the act, and no matter whether it is known or unknown by others, it is of everlasting value. We may confidently approach each decision knowing that it does matter and it does have meaning. Our spiritual affirmation becomes, I know that this moment is of great value—a pearl of great price.

A helpful image which gathers up these affirmations is that of God surrounding us. Our every moment begins with

God's new possibility for that event, continues with God's embracing presence with us, and concludes with God's cherishing that moment everlastingly: God before us, God with us, God after us. With Brother Lawrence we engage in "The Practice of the Presence of God."

Prayer has been a traditional spiritual discipline of the faithful, and so it is central in this vision of God as well. There are, naturally, some variations from the tradition. Given all that has been said, we do not have to ask God to be present with us, a petition which is made in many dinner invocations. We need not invoke God to be with us, for God is present. We can count on God's constancy. The more appropriate request is to ask for awareness of God's presence: "May we be open." "May we be aware." "May we listen."

Another variation is that we need not ask for God's guidance. As we have been exploring in these pages, God always offers direction. Each moment of our lives begins with such direction. Again, the important petition is to ask for openness to hear and respond to that direction. One simple form of prayer is, May I be aware of your possibility for this moment, and may I be willing to act upon it. A shorter version, comparable to the more traditional "flash prayer" is, Who would you have me to be in this next moment?

Rather than techniques of prayer, the important focus is upon the relationship in which prayer occurs. If we are in conversation with the Graceful One who fully understands us and affirms us, who offers new direction which is for our beauty and the beauty of the world, and who cherishes everlastingly every decision we make, then we may ask ourselves what we would like to share with such a person. This relationship invites sharing from the depth, as deep calls unto deep. One need not be an orator, poet, or saint, merely authentic and responsive. Prayer is speaking freely.

72

We began with thinking which led to imaging which in turn overflowed into practicing. Each needs the other. Each grows out of the other and flows back to enrich the other. Imaging promotes certain practices; practices influence changes in images. We are now finished with setting the stage and are ready to begin the action.

Each of the chapters in the next section illustrates the activity of the Caring Friend in the council meeting. The stories focus upon different council members, offering an enriched understanding of their activities. Hopefully, the council meeting will come alive more fully when clothed in realistic human situations.

To capture our humanness, each story has the title of a feeling state with which we might identify. There is a certain flow in the order in which each story appears. As preparation, a short preview of the ten dramas follows.

"Divided" gives a feel for the multitude of council members who come together when the question of which car to buy is the agenda for De and Eric. Some visible, others shadowy, still others invisible, they gather to deliberate. By means of the process of my mother's senility, "Loss" illustrates the profound influence of changes in the physical body upon the possibilities God may offer. The characters in the drama are the Caring Friend and a disabled council member.

"Helpless" records the fiery childhood moment in which I decided that I must be a coward and the ways that I kept proving it to myself through the years. A council member, like this one representing the past, has tremendous power, but the Caring Friend lured me beyond this crippling vision. "Choosing" is where this book began and holds a particularly fond place in my heart. My tussle between the past Roberts and the new possibility for Robert, the burger-eaters versus the salad-eater, portrays the process of an ordinary council meeting. The emphasis here is upon what goes on in a council meeting rather than who is there, as was described earlier with De and Eric.

"Trapped" takes one of Ann's most frequent yet most upsetting daily habits—smoking—to show God's involvement in the small areas of life. Ann's pathway to being a nonsmoker was to develop and strengthen who she could become, the area of potential where the Caring Friend lures within each council meeting. "Changing" starts with Susan's repulsion for a particular hymn and moves her to increasing appreciation of those words. In a fantasy journey she comes to see that she has an inheritance from the world's past and that God persuaded others then just as God now persuades her.

"Puzzled" eavesdrops on a conversation between Marge and her teen-aged daughter, Jan, showing that when the model of a persuasive God is followed a new style of parenting emerges. If the Caring Friend is empathic with Marge and offers her possibilities, then she could risk being empathic with Jan. "Ignoring" outlines the vision which guides Joyce as she thinks about the unthinkable—nuclear holocaust. The persuasive love moving at the center of the universe leads her to differ with those who would welcome such an event as Armageddon, those who believe God will not allow it to happen, and those who have only their own resources to prevent it.

"Dying" is a letter which I sent to my wife's aunt—a letter in which I strongly desire to give her what I have. As I sat in my office composing the letter, I was surprised at how the features of my own faith poured out. I concluded that perhaps it is only when called for that all we have experienced and learned in bits and pieces springs forth woven together. "Adjusting" describes my moment-by-moment prayer for God's possibilities as the snow piled deeper and deeper, thwarting my well-made travel plans. The council meetings I held ranged from peaceful certainty to utter mob scene as I encountered each rapidly changing situation.

So, let the actors and actresses speak for themselves. The stage is set; the props are in place. Raise the curtain!

III.

Trying Out the Answer:

God Within the Ordinary and the Dramatic

7.

Divided: The Station Wagon or the Four-Door?

*I*T was over the second cup of coffee on Saturday mornings that De and Eric solved many problems. The agenda today was a car, a concern which had been brewing for a long time. Slipping on the ice while bending and twisting to buckle James into the rear seat while Jennifer and Heather stood juggling the heavy grocery sacks had been the last straw for De. They had outgrown their two-door compact. Something had to be done now.

With paper and pencil in hand, De and Eric listed what they needed. More room was at the top of the list. Monthly payments followed close behind. Soon they discovered that they needed two lists—one for needs and the other for wants. Needs were the obvious ones: a station wagon or a full-sized sedan with a large trunk, four doors, manageable monthly payments, a heavy and safe rig, a new or late-model vehicle, reasonable gas mileage, good tires, low maintenance, and a fair resale value. They were satisfied with their discovery of all they should take into account.

Wants were considered but were less important. They

each had personal preferences for a certain make, model, styling, upholstery, type of transmission, and color. Impulse and feelings were to be included along with all their well-reasoned needs. They had owned enough cars before to know that it is not easy to drive a fully practical car you don't like.

In making the list there were bursts of talk and ideas which flowed faster than the hand could write. Then there were the lulls and quietness in which they seemed to reach a plateau after climbing mountains. Those times led to one or the other saying, "Well, now what?"

A new flurry of talk occurred when De suggested they make a new list of what was best for the children. In the process they found that it was neither easy to separate their needs from their children's nor always possible to put themselves in their children's shoes and guess their needs. This task was definitely more difficult than asking themselves what they needed or wanted.

They saw future birthday parties, slumber parties, and softball games where a wagon would be helpful. They saw growing needs for other material things, requiring that they keep monthly payments down. Safety belts were already foremost among their needs, as was space for play which avoids the teasing and tears that can distract a driver or spoil a vacation trip. Both agreed that the children were years distant from becoming drivers, so that a new set of needs could be met with a future car.

Again, the question arose, "So, what else do we need to put down on our list?" They faced another quiet lull.

De and Eric each illustrate what a council meeting looks like. The first council meeting began with one person thinking about the car, an event which is complex in its own right. Sitting down together, each of their council meetings now includes the perspectives of another person. From one person, the council grows to two, and from two to five. They have listened to themselves, to one another, and now to their three children. A five-member council has gathered—Eric, De, Jennifer, Heather, and James.

Up to this point the council meeting is not that unusual. The obvious people whom most of us would take into account in the decision to buy a car are present and represented. Most would include one's marriage partner and children in such a major decision. Most would give some thought to the future as well as the present. Yet, in fact, the picture so far shows only a small fraction of the council members actually present. Seated in council chairs among the five family members there are a number of much less obvious, probably even invisible and unheard, members present at each meeting.

It is these who will be allowed to speak now simply to show how large and complex most of our council meetings are. Members will not be allowed to dialogue and confront one another as in an actual meeting; they will simply introduce themselves and offer their perspectives on the decision at hand. The characters of the play will be introduced, but the drama will not unfold.

Let us now imagine the wider, less obvious, only partly conscious circle of council members within De and Eric. If we listen carefully we can eavesdrop on their words.

"I think you should buy a smooth-riding and heavy station wagon which is comfortable for long-distance traveling. A wagon allows plenty of space for luggage and room for the children to play on a long trip" (Council Member: Eric's mother, who lives five hundred miles away).

"I urge you to look carefully at the latest reports on the gas mileage and maintenance record of the models you are considering. In addition, I suggest that you buy your car before December 31 to gain the sales-tax deduction on your income tax" (Council Member: De and Eric's accountant).

"What's the big deal? Figure out what you want and go plunk down your money. You work hard. You bring home the bacon. You deserve to have what you want. Don't be a wimp and listen to everybody else!" (Council Member: a co-worker at the telephone company).

"I suggest that you consider the car that is a balance between your basic needs and a fair price. I say that simply so that you don't get so strapped by your monthly payments that you haven't much money left to do other things. I have seen too many couples with young children become car poor" (Council Member: De and Eric's pastor).

"I guess I've worked on all of them. You would be wise to get one that you can do many of the repairs on yourself. I know you can save a lot by changing your own oil and doing your own tune-ups. I would advise you to get a simple one. In the long run, I think you would be happier with it" (Council Member: service station owner where De and Eric trade).

"In my twenty years of being in the business, I've seen a lot of them pass through here. Right now I'm really sold on the van. You get the room you need and the gas mileage is super. In summer you have the pop-top for camping, and in winter it's great for packing the skis. You can't go wrong on a rig like this." (Council Member: salesperson at a local van dealership).

"Now, I surely don't want to throw cold water on your plans, but with the interest rates as they are now I would certainly encourage you to consider a late-model used car. As I look over your house payments and other credit charges, I am aware that the highest loan we could make might be less than what you have been thinking about" (Council Member: loan officer at their bank).

"I really think you would be wise to buy from one of the big three. We Americans have got to support other Americans. If you don't buy from American automakers, I may be laid off in three weeks or maybe six months. I need work. I've got kids to raise just like you, and I need you people to help me out" (Council Member: Pittsburgh steelworker).

"Stay away from those foreign cars. Every time you buy one, you undercut us. Sure they can do it, because they've got all that cheap labor. Don't we deserve good pay just as much as you and the rest of the people in this country? We've got to stick together. This country was built on taking care of our own!" (Council Member: union representative, United Auto Workers).

"I don't know how it all fits together. Everything is so complicated today, but I do know that we need to earn a living. I don't understand why, if we can build a car and ship it overseas for a cheaper price, you should not buy our car. We too are a family, we too have hopes for our children, we too want to share in the good things of life" (Council Member: spouse of a worker at a Japanese automobile manufacturer).

"About all I know is that when this oil rig runs, I work. When I work, I get paid. I advise you to buy a car that will continue to use our crude oil to make your gasoline. If you stop driving, I don't work, and I don't get paid" (Council Member: twenty-five-year-old worker on an oil rig off the coast of Nigeria).

"I find it hard to understand your decision. Even in my wildest dreams, I cannot imagine having a car; I will probably never own a bicycle. I simply hope that my body will keep healthy and I won't be burdened by another pregnancy so that I can work in the fields. We must have a good harvest this year so that our village can survive through the rainy season. Your decision seems to be one of convenience, while mine is one of survival. I don't know your world" (Council Member: subsistence farmer in a Third World nation).

"I would like to grow up in a place where I can see the nearby San Gabriel Mountains, breathe freely of fresh air, and watch the stars on a pleasant summer evening" (Council Member: a fetus developing in the womb of a twenty-two-year-old woman living in West Covina, California).

"I want to live. I want to soar through clear, clean air. I want to feed on the berries and seeds of healthy trees and plants. I hope that you will consider my needs in your choice, yet I have few ways to influence your decision" (Council Member: an English sparrow living in a blue spruce about two blocks from Interstate 5 in Seattle).

"I am a part of your scenery at breakfast each morning. I fill a basic need for you by providing oxygen which you must have for continuing life. When I am surrounded by too much carbon monoxide, I find it exceedingly difficult to produce that oxygen. I urge you to consider an automobile that will not overwhelm me with its exhaust fumes so that we can continue to cooperate in the balance of life" (Council Member: a Red Delicious apple tree on Grover Avenue in East Wenatchee, Washington).

"I can only echo what I have heard from others who have wanted dearly to cooperate with you, yet who fear that they will be maimed by the waste products of your car. I wonder how much I can handle and at what point I may be utterly overwhelmed" (Council Member: an atom of nitrogen in a vegetable garden plot on Red Apple Road).

The wider circle speaks. Among them is one unique voice luring De and Eric to listen to all of the beloved.

8.

Loss: Mom's Getting Senile

*I*N technical language it is Organic Brain Syndrome, more specifically, Primary Degenerative Dementia. In human language it is painful loss. In council meeting language it is a disabled council. The body, as member of the council, is no longer fully functioning.

Those are the formal words for what my mother went through. Depending upon who was speaking, the process was described as getting senile, losing her mind, or playing without a full deck of cards. One medical book says that Primary Degenerative Dementia is a multifaceted loss of intellectual ability. Its onset is usually slow, almost unnoticeable, but slowly and relentlessly it brings death over a period of several years.

Looking back, there were certainly signs of this slow onset. In our telephone conversations my mother would say strange things. "They're after me. They're trying to get me." We both knew she had lived alone for years; nevertheless, she told me about the strange people in the house. Even more puzzling, she would say, "Let me go, Bob. Don't try to keep me here." Then there would be silence on the other end of the line, except for the sound of the television in the background. The telephone had been left dangling.

Visiting us, she became so agitated that I reluctantly agreed to drive her back home on my birthday. She was adamant about buying me a gift on our trip home, but during that day totally forgot her desire and even forgot that it was my birthday. In a later visit to her home, I saw other signs— food left too long in the refrigerator and now becoming moldy, pans soaking in the sink obviously blackened by some forgetful accident.

The following summer I received an emergency call that neighbors had found my mother in a coma. She was now recuperating in the hospital. The barking of her dog behind the closed bedroom shades gave neighbors a clue that something was wrong. Mom had not been keeping the necessary balance between her eating and her insulin. The result was a diabetic coma. Her physician told us that she should no longer live alone, so we arranged for her to be transferred to a convalescent center there. If there had been subtle clues before, they were blatantly evident now. In her home there were pathways through disorder.

During that visit we arranged for my mother to live in a private home with a couple who supervised several elderly people. Our relief at having her settled in a homelike atmosphere was short-lived. Within the next two months we learned that this setting was proving to be impossible. Mom was walking away trying to get back to her home, undressing in public, and flushing money down the toilet.

In late November, my younger brother flew with our mother to Wenatchee. Our home was a brief stopping point before taking her to a convalescent center in Cashmere, eleven miles away. That evening remains one of my most vivid memories of loss. Tears welled up as I looked at the small gray-haired woman sitting in the front seat of the car, mute and staring blankly into space. I could scarcely believe that this person before me was my mother.

The medical book says that memory impairment is usually the most prominent symptom. In severe cases, a person may forget names, telephone numbers, directions, conversations, and the events of the day. In advanced forms persons forget the names of close relatives, their occupation, schooling, birthday, or occasionally even their own name.

My mother had a bouncy spirit and a strong little body, and the regular routine, nutritious food, and gentle care helped her to recuperate greatly. However, she was forgetful! At different times I might be her father, husband, or beau. The scowling look she sometimes gave my wife, Adrienne, as we were visiting told me that on that day I was husband or beau. I would never hear her call me son or Bob again.

She talked often to the nurses and aides about the baby she had lost over fifty years earlier — as though it had just happened! At times she recognized her cherished red station wagon, and at other times she had no awareness whatsoever of which car in the parking lot was hers. One day one of our friends asked her where she lived. She unhesitatingly replied, "153 Lincoln Street, just like always."

Ten minutes after we had taken her out to lunch she did not recall that we had even been to visit. She could not tell us whether or not she had eaten breakfast, what she had eaten, or if she had taken her medication. Some moments were humorous, others pathetic. It became familiar to feel sick to my stomach and get a lump in my throat as we drove back to the convalescent center after an outing. Once again we would go through our painful parting. She would ask why we were stopping here, fully convinced that we had come to take her back home.

In the disease, abstract thinking becomes impaired. A

person cannot cope with novel tasks and neglects personal appearance and hygiene. Both traits are evidence of poor judgment and impulse control.

Taking my mother to lunch became one of our visiting rituals. Unable to order from the menu, she would have whatever I did. It was distressing to watch her begin to pour catsup over her entire plate of food, especially since I could recall her former meticulous manners. During one meal at the center, we observed my mother take her spoon, dip it into the chocolate pudding, and put it into her bowl of split-pea soup. She left her dentures in another resident's room. Later, after misplacing them several more times, they were completely lost. Her eyeglasses followed the same course. Such incidents brought her loss home vividly, for we remembered that for years she had kept an eye on a classroom of children. Now, however, she was unable to watch over her own personal effects.

Another symptom of dementia is that people may wander and become lost. In Twin Falls, she found her way back to her Lincoln Street home. During her first winter in Cashmere, she walked away one cold night and could certainly have died of exposure had she not been found stumbling through the snow by a neighbor. Aides came to know her as "the wandering one." When asked where she was going, she replied, "Ely, Nevada" — her childhood home.

Personality change is almost invariably present in dementia. It can involve either an alteration or an accentuation of a person's natural traits. For instance, a normally active person becomes increasingly apathetic and withdrawn.

In the midst of the pain that I experienced, my mother's personality change was one of the positive highlights. In my youth I knew my mother as one who, though normally kind, could become enraged instantly with little provocation. I learned, thereby, to be cautious around her. Surprisingly, in her senility, she became a pleasant person. She was exceedingly cooperative, smiled amiably, and expressed thanks for each small helping act. With the passage of time one of the few modes of communication left between us was to smile at one another across the lunch table. I came to accept those smiles as her highest possibility for those moments.

Finally, when dementia becomes severe, the individual may be virtually mute and eventually totally oblivious to his or her surroundings and require constant care.

As weeks turned into months, my mother could no longer dress herself or get ready for bed. She became incontinent during the night. Diapers were necessary, and a harness was required to keep her in bed through the night. She would sit quietly in a sunny dayroom for long periods of time, saying nothing. Even the television program seemed invisible and silent to her. Watching, I wondered if there were activity going on within, for there was so little occurring outside. She retained the important word *Yes*, her response when asked if she wanted another cup of coffee or some dessert at lunch. For one who had taught children to read, uttering only this three-letter word represented radical loss.

During her second winter at the center, Mom suffered a series of small strokes. She lay unconscious and breathing erratically. Standing by her tiny form in the hospital bed, I was moved once again to tears. I felt her nearing death. In fact, however, within weeks she recovered and was returned to the center.

Our final sharing with my mother was lunch the day before Christmas of the following year. In the next two weeks she failed quickly. Having been told that she was rapidly declining, Adrienne and I went to her bedside. It was evident that she was entering her final hours of life. We placed our hands on hers, spoke gently that she had our permission to go, and prayed the Lord's Prayer. She died peacefully the next afternoon.

I trust that God was present during these five years of gradual loss, as close to my mother as her very breath, persuading, understanding, comforting, and cherishing. Because of this trust, I was spared the questions which so frequently accompany painful loss and which are usually clothed in disappointment, blame, or anger. Why did God allow it? Why didn't God do something? The heartbreak was enough without the added burden of these heartbreaking questions.

This form of questioning grows out of an understanding of God as one who controls everything and can do anything. In contrast, the council meeting portrays a God who is persuading within a council, and in this case, a disabled council. The new question emerges as, What possibilities can God offer to a limited council? The body is a necessary and prominent member of the council. How it is present affects what God can offer and ultimately what the council can accomplish.

In my view, God had been persuading my mother since her conception through each of the many changes her body would undergo. God offered new and appropriate possibilities to the fetus, infant, child, adolescent, young adult, mature woman, and elderly woman. Never had God been absent from a council meeting in all of my mother's years of development.

During her elderly years, when arteries became gradually narrowed and hardened, like logs forming a logjam in a river, her brain was not adequately nourished. God was affected by these changes and had to relate to the new physical conditions. It was as if the body had elected new representatives to be members of the council, and God had

90

to relate to those newly elected members. God was doing what the conditions allowed God to do.

While the conditions affected God, at the same time God was continually influencing and urging those very conditions in critically important directions. God must have persuaded my mother thousands upon thousands of times to make healthy decisions. Those persuasions might have taken the form of vigorously exercising her body regularly and creatively modifying her eating habits. Possibilities were, no doubt, offered.

As with all persons, however, my mother was the one who decided which possibilities were to be given life. She was overweight her entire adult life, smoked periodically during my boyhood years, and showed little awareness of fat and sugar in her diet. In later life, she developed diabetes. God's lure toward health was obviously only partly heeded. God was surely a persuasive voice in each of my mother's decisions but not the final cause of her health or illness.

There is yet another place where we can look for God's activity. We need a microscope, however; for the site is the cells making up my mother's body. They too have their own council meetings. Like persons, cells can create only with what they have, so they must respond to their surroundings. If they are bathed frequently in nutritious fluids, they can become something more than if they are regularly flooded by harmful solutions.

So it must have been also with the build-up of plaque in the arteries. Cells composing that artery had to be created under the condition of this growing deposit. God persuades, but tissue damage is real and often irreversible. There is a point of no return. God offered appropriate lures to a disabled council at the cellular level too.

In my mother's apparently monotonous and routine

91

existence during her last months, there were significant opportunities in simple acts for God to open her awareness to rich pleasures: the snugness of the bed covers tucked gently around her shoulders, the smoothness of the pudding placed in her mouth, the warmth of the bubble bath on her skin, and the security of a firm hand clasping hers.

As for the rest of my family, I am confident that God lured us to accept reality as it emerged. Moving from mourning our loss, we were gradually able to accept my mother just as she was in that moment. Each new loss changed what we were able to do. We learned to be satisfied with her silence and her childlike eating. We reached the point where it seemed that all there was left to do was to smile at her, hug her, and massage her hands. We did so with acceptance.

In the final months of her life, this shell of a person was surely no longer my mother. Before me was a familiar body but not the same person. The mother I had known, who had raised three sons largely by herself, had earned a college degree two months after I had, and had taught a generation of children, was now absent. Still, I held to the hope that all of her accomplishments of previous years were now saved and cherished within the life of God.

I experienced the loss of my mother, but the person of my mother had not been lost.

9.

Helpless: The Coward

I WAS horrified by the sights and sounds before me. As I stood there, I felt a terrible pulling in two directions—one urging that I lunge at my father to help my brother, the other holding me safely where I was. This tearing conflict went on for what seemed an eternity, but in reality was probably only minutes. I stood frozen in my tracks. With all the intensity that I possessed, I held onto my mother's leg.

My father had chased my older brother into the basement, where he was now trapped. Frantically, my mother and I had followed, racing down the stairs. Now through terrorized eyes, I watched my father angrily beating my brother with a broom handle.

In this fiery moment, I called myself a coward. This decision would continue to define me for the next thirty-five years of my life. My brother had been in trouble and I should have helped him. I didn't. I had let my brother down. I felt terribly guilty. I had explained all this to myself by saying, "I must be a coward."

In that moment, there emerged a design which would

guide my life. The design included a definition: I am a coward; an action: I let people down; and a feeling: I feel guilty. This powerful definition of myself, which was the center of the design, would be a prominent voice in all future decisions.

I was a five-year-old. My brother was eighteen months older and my younger brother was one. My mother was eighteen years younger than my fifty-five-year-old father. In relationship to these particular people, in that particular house, on that particular occasion, I came to a decision about myself. In this context, the coward was born.

As each month and year passed, I largely unknowingly created new ways to be a coward in each newly emerging situation. When we played house, I always chose to be the brother, never the father. When my older brother was out-doors picking fights with the neighborhood Mormon and Catholic kids, I was helping Mom in the house.

Although I am now physically the largest of the three sons, I always managed to allow my older brother to win our fights. I will always bear an unsightly V-shaped scar on my left forearm as an unpleasant reminder of anger at my brother, which I feared to unleash on him, but which I did send shattering through a glass window. Add to this picture one who has never been able to stand the sight of blood, especially when someone approached with a needle with the intent of drawing blood, and my cowardice was confirmed.

I was quite certain that girls would not like someone as cowardly as I, and I usually made that happen. It was not that I turned out for football and failed; I never even considered that I could play football.

Guilt continued to be a prominent feeling as I let people down, defining myself repeatedly as inadequate. I experienced these feelings and this definition of myself intensely with my mother. She was continually unhappy in her life situation, and I continually let her down by somehow not making her happy. In situations where I was supposed to be out having fun, I would feel guilt knowing that, wherever she was, my mother was feeling lonely and unhappy.

Throughout my college and adult years, the coward continued to weave himself into each new event. In those moments where one is called upon to act confidently and boldly, the coward spoke most fluently. I was painfully tense and tight when dancing with a young woman. The instructor of the college social dancing class once asked out of dire frustration if I were a boxer. She saw me time and again leading with my right. I dreaded dancing with a new partner for fear that I would fail once again and let her down. In both church and college choirs, I chose the cautious route of following the lead of the baritone seated next to me.

When I worked as a youth counselor in the church, I was told that I was "playing with the kids," and I complied by interpreting my job as not being "manly." Such work did not match the hard-hat construction job or the highway survey crew where many college friends worked during the summer.

During my graduate school years I unhappily wore the label of professional student and felt like one who could not make it in the real world. As a counselor-in-training, I eagerly embraced the newly emerging client-centered counseling, with its emphasis upon listening and understanding, in contrast to teaching or speaking with authority. In teaching college students on several occasions, I enjoyed the lecturing but hated the grading. The coward did not want to evaluate a student. As senior minister of a church, I quickly formed a co-ministry with the associate minister. While believing in the venture, I am also sure that the coward was lurking behind that decision.

There were also the everyday events in which I brought the coward into play repeatedly. I did not want to call the

95

baby-sitter. I remained as frozen in my recliner chair as I had on the basement steps years before when solicitors rang the doorbell. I dreaded confronting the maintenance person who put de-icer on the snowy sidewalks, badly staining the office carpets.

In all of these events I was repeatedly defining myself as the coward, letting people down, and feeling guilty for doing so. It began to dawn on me that I set up situations so that I would once again prove the truth of my five-year-old decision. I did all the things on my list for the day, except one. I returned all the telephone calls for the morning, except one. I dictated all the letters, except the letter of recommendation requiring that I evaluate someone. In each new situation that I entered and in each new relationship that I formed, I allowed myself to repeat in some variation the theme of coward in action. It became second nature and most often barely in my awareness.

Facts about myself that did not fit with being a coward could not chip away at the label, which seemed etched in granite. That I earned high grades in college prompted me to think that I was a hard-working coward. That there were girls and young women who did like me made me wonder about their taste.

I was elected to offices in high school and college. I did earn three graduate degrees. As a pastor, I led a congregation in completing a new building, and I did prove to my two career Army officer brothers that I, too, could "take it" by surviving Marine Corps boot camp. Like my father before me, I did develop my own business. Reading the outward accomplishments of my autobiography, one would hardly guess that within there lived a coward. None of these accomplishments, however, called into question my decision at five years old.

At the age of forty, with the help of a skilled and caring

professional, I first questioned this label. Looking back at the early event, I was able to reinterpret what had happened. I was able to see what I did not see then. Rather than being a coward, I had acted with wisdom! In that impossible moment I had protected the most precious possession I had—my own capacities. I realized that it had been a healthy decision to stand on the stairway rather than throw myself into the foray. I even came to see that God may have been luring me to keep my hand tightly gripped around my mother's leg.

Why I did not come to this new insight sooner is unclear. Surely God had persuaded me thousands of times to break out of this self-created mold. Perhaps God lured me away from being more of the coward than I was. Somehow, in the protection of a group and the safety of a capable leader, the Caring Friend must have reached out to me and spoken powerfully, "Rise and walk!"

In the burst of this new understanding, the past lost its firm hold. No longer need I define myself ever anew as coward in each emerging occasion. Rather, I was now free to experiment, to see who I might become in each new setting. The chains were broken; the prisoner was released.

Still, there are times of guilt and occasions when I feel I have let someone down. Nevertheless, it is possible for me now to stop, think, and reconsider if I really want to do that to myself. In any new setting now, I have the option of allowing myself to "fly by automatic pilot" or to define myself in a new way. New possibilities are heard and seen in each council meeting.

These pages from my own autobiography are offered to illustrate the heavy influence of one's personal past, especially the way that a child defines himself or herself. Such definitions have phenomenal power. Consider weak, ugly, stupid, unlovable, or flawed. Each of these labels, like mine, is born in some specific moment that is often an accumulation of painful moments. In that instant, a new voice enters the council meeting of that person, a voice that may become dominant in all future events.

Although the coward still lives and is still a part of my council meetings, he seldom chairs the meeting!

10.

Choosing: Now, What Will I Order for Lunch Today?

*T*HE hostess greets us with a smile and asks, "Two for lunch?" I nod. She selects two menus and asks us to follow her. I feel a bounce in my step as I move from the tiled entryway to the softly carpeted dining room. I catch bits of conversation as I walk by those already seated. A rising voice here, a burst of laughter there, the clatter of dishes being cleared from the table, and the tinkling of ice water being poured into a glass fill the room with familiar restaurant sounds. The ever-present coffee aroma drifts through the room.

Passing each table, I steal a glance at the lunches that have already been served. All increase the hunger that I already felt as I entered the restaurant. We arrive at our booth. The fabric on the cushion feels soft to my touch. The hostess opens a menu and places it in my hands. She repeats the same for my friend and departs with "Enjoy your lunch."

I follow my old habit of looking at the whole menu before getting down to particulars. I like to get the big picture. I scan quickly, looking at the price then crossing back to the entree. I am a right-sided menu reader.

I feel disappointment when my favorite tuna melt sandwich is no longer listed. It is like meeting an old friend again when I see the peanut-butter-and-jelly sandwich. I regret that it is listed in the section for the Under-10 Crowd. I sense a familiar revulsion when I see the steak sandwich. The lasagna divides me into feelings of wanting it but counting it too rich for lunch. I balk at the price of the salmon filet.

Hurdling quickly over the salads listed, I feel tense when I see the "Cup and a Half," a cup of soup and one-half sandwich. It would never fill me up. Moving on, I remember that the patty melt was too greasy the last time I ordered it.

Then my friend calls my attention to the special of the day. The small white card clipped to the menu reads:

Double Burger with Salad and Fries

> Two delicious quarter-pound beef patties in a large sesame seed bun, served with tomato, pickles, and onion. A fresh green salad and a healthy serving of golden-brown french fries.

Not bad! I may have discovered today's lunch. The price is right. As the special it should come quickly. There would be no waiting around feeling my hunger pangs grow. I should be filled. The beef should stick to my ribs until dinner, so there would be no danger of hunger later. A good dash of catsup could enhance the taste of the beef.

Here is the council meeting in action during a most routine event. For many middle-class Americans there is surely nothing unusual or dramatic about ordering lunch. Still, the event illustrates the power of the many facets of one's personal past. How these council members, who represent different stages of the past, enter into a lively tension with a new possibility is the purpose of this inner view of lunch. God is ever present in the ordinary as the bringer of new possibilities which seek to transform even the most firmly rooted habits.

It is as though a committee is meeting within, and I must get at least a majority vote before I can place my order. Each committee member appears to bring his own concern. Is it cheap? Is it fast? Will it fill me? Will it stick with me? Does it taste good? Is it good for me? While not being the ideal answer to every question, the double burger could get the nod of the committee.

As I hear each committee member in this moment, I recognize the voices of earlier Roberts. In the distant past is the little boy Robert. Many is the time he followed his older brother to their father's chair after dinner to have his well-filled tummy patted while reciting "full up." Thinking he could not stand to feel hunger, the grade-school Robert interrupted the neighborhood basketball game to make and quickly devour a peanut-butter-and-jelly sandwich. This same Robert hid chocolate cupcakes in his desk at school to quell immediately any hunger which might develop there.

A junior-high Robert, who lived on a cattle ranch, was repulsed and nauseated while helping to butcher a heifer, while the teenager lived on hamburgers, fries, and milkshakes, using catsup to disguise the beef taste. The already price-conscious Robert intensified his concern during low-budget college-student years. The adult Robert laced up his running shoes and joined the joggers. The mature Robert became increasingly concerned with the impact of producing different foods upon the world ecology.

I am certainly not a blank sheet upon which each entree writes its message; rather I project myself onto the pages of the menu. I dance with each entree. But it is even more complicated than that, for I seem to bring a number of me's

101

into the decision. The Roberts of my past are present, ready to guide.

I breathe a deep sigh of relief that today I won't have to go through the tennis match, the merry-go-round, or the frozen stalemate I sometimes endure when I study a menu. Most of the committee agreed on the special.

Just when I think that the issue is settled, a strange thought comes to me: "How about a salad?" The idea was really far-out. It was so unlike me that my first reaction was, "You've got to be kidding! *Me*, eat a salad!"

My second reaction is one of wondering. I become intrigued by the idea. Surely, there are some merits to the thought even though it is so foreign. Then I start bouncing back and forth between calling it ridiculous and toying with it. What I thought would be a simple decision has now become vastly more complicated. I look at the menu again, this time reading it slowly:

Turkey Breast Salad

> Slices of moist white turkey on a bed of crisp lettuce, garnished with tomato slices, asparagus spears, and a dill pickle. Choice of dressings. Just right for the smaller appetite or the weight watcher.

The new idea of eating a salad has a different feeling to it. I have no earlier Robert who was an avid salad eater, so I can't possibly feel the same way as I do about a peanut-butter-and-jelly sandwich. This is different. In fact, in my history a salad was always a small plate to the left of the dinner plate and was eaten before the main course. I have no past to guide me here.

I do not simply dismiss the idea but begin to weigh it more carefully. I feel hesitant. The idea carries threat with it.

Long-standing beliefs that I must get full at every meal and that I cannot stand hunger are being questioned.

I move from being threatened to a more balanced position. A salad is, after all, a healthy choice. A salad would be good for me. On the other hand, I would probably have to wait longer for it. The price is higher. Should I spend more for fewer calories? The taste of lettuce can never match that of the burger and fries. What bothers me most of all is the phrase about "smaller appetite."

Even while these thoughts are forming, the resistance emerges again with great power. I'll never get full on that! I'll be caved in by four o'clock! What will I do then? I don't have any goodies stashed away at the office. Besides, a salad is no fun!

Another thought intrudes. Wouldn't I be proud of myself if I could order less and not overeat? Fear had governed me for a long time. Perhaps I could be a person who is in control of his eating. Maybe I could be one who eats less food, accepts the feeling of a partly full stomach, and copes with hunger as it comes. Maybe I could!

Just as I begin to imagine myself in this new way, a wave of feeling rolls over me washing away that picture. Salad is simply not real food like meat, potatoes, and bread. Real food fills and satisfies.

Once again the idea of me as a salad eater comes softly tiptoeing back again. A strange picture, indeed! It does fit better with my beliefs. Less is required from the earth to provide turkeys and vegetables. But I had never pictured myself as a salad eater before. I struggle: burger eater or salad eater? Who will Robert become today?

The earlier Roberts are challenged by a unique voice in their very midst. To be sure the voice is neither familiar nor vigorously applauded. On the contrary, tension and conflict emerges. The Roberts who had provided direction in so many earlier eating decisions are threatened now by the voice of a mysterious intruder. Gradually, however, the ideas of the more recent Roberts begin to find some common ground with the strange possibility.

I risk. Turning to the waitress, I announce, "I'll try the turkey salad." I decide to be a salad eater — well, almost anyway. I decide on a wheat roll to go along with the salad, an insurance policy against hunger later. It could be said that a new Robert wins the day, but not without some influence from all the earlier Roberts. A blending has emerged.

As I make the decision, I cannot predict the future. Perhaps the discomfort of hungry moments this afternoon will result in this being the one and only time that I will be a salad eater at lunch. On the other hand, it may be the birth of a new Robert who will grow in strength and gradually become a powerful guiding voice. I know only that I will try being unfamiliar in a most familiar situation.

11.

Trapped: I'm a Smoker and I Hate It

ANN smoked and wanted desperately to stop. The problem was especially upsetting because she was a nurse and knew firsthand the harmful results of smoking. Try as she would, however, she couldn't stop. She knew all the right reasons, even said them all to patients, but none convinced her. She had about decided that she was a weak-willed person, a none-too-happy conclusion.

Where was God in Ann's struggle? She found it hard to imagine God being involved at all in such a small matter. In contrast, the answer offered here is that God was deeply involved with her. Each puff of a cigarette, probably occurring 360 or more times a day, is of utmost importance to God. Strange as it may seem, God does not have more important things to do. What persons decide to do moment by moment is of deep significance to God. Let us see how that can be so.

The council-meeting image offers Ann a new view of herself. She may have decided to be a smoker 3,537,986 times, but that is vastly different than saying, "I am a smoker." Each time she called herself a smoker she gave more power to the name. That's who she was! If so, then Ann was trapped. If, however, Ann saw herself as a decision-maker in each new smoking event, then she could also picture herself changing. "I am" is clearly not the same as "I have decided."

This is not to imply that such change was easy. The heavy hand of the past weighed heavily on her shoulder. The most natural thing to do in any new moment was to repeat what she had done thousands of times before. Habits are real and powerful, but habits are not what totally determined what Ann did in the next moment. They were but strong voices among a number of other voices.

It was craver versus scolder. The craver craved a cigarette, and the scolder scolded during and after that cigarette. Ann fought with herself. She kept herself deeply divided.

She was fully aware of her need to hurry off the hospital floor to the nurse's lounge for a cigarette, to leave her son's basketball game during halftime to join other smokers outside the gym door, and to fidget through a meeting just waiting to reach her car and light up. Ann was equally aware of her shortness of breath hurrying from a patient's side to the nurse's station, the pain in her lungs on last summer's hikes, and the nagging and persistent cough each morning.

Ann also knew the future of smoking. She, more than any other, had seen the many patients who suffered serious heart problems and others who now lived with a portable oxygen tank as a constant companion. She knew the likelihood of an extremely limited future ahead.

From painful experience she had learned that "Don'ts" don't work. She had put herself through a full measure of lectures and scoldings. For a short time they appeared to curb her smoking, only to crumble soon after in a time of great stress or a lack of concentration. Although she felt trapped by her habit, she had had no success breaking out of it by slapping her own hands.

106

Interestingly enough, the real need was for new possibilities offered by the Caring Friend to transform each voice — the craver and the scolder. No small task, indeed, but still a task which could happen with Ann's cooperation.

A beginning was to take each voice in turn and understand it as a positive need rather than a fighting enemy. At first glance it was difficult to consider the craving voice as positive, but it became possible by tracing the history of earlier events.

There was a time when Ann did not smoke, and there was the moment when Ann first smoked. This was a crucial moment and was clearly one in which she saw smoking as a solution to some problem, an answer to some need. Viewing it in this way allowed her to see it as an act which was not necessarily bad, evil, or mysterious; rather, it was an answer in her particular situation.

For some it is a need to belong to the group or show independence from parents. For others it is an answer to unbearable pressure and stress. For still others it is a reason to relax and so it was for Ann. In her family it was important to be doing something all the time, avoiding at any cost just sitting around. The question she faced was, What do you do if you want to stop doing your chores but have absolutely no good reason for doing so? After many tries, Ann found a reason. She could sit down and still be doing something — smoke! She felt a relief in finding this answer.

In fact, Ann did relax in smoking. Though not aware of it, she did breathe more deeply as she inhaled. Moreover, she was not aware at that time that she could have gained most of the benefits without the cigarette. Nonetheless, it is this relaxation which was needed, craved, and acted upon time and again. Desiring relaxation is a positive need.

Many council meetings followed after the one in which the first cigarette was smoked. Ann gained pleasure and her habit was strengthened with each puff, as many as three hundred to five hundred times a day. Times, places, and situations were increasingly associated with smoking.

Her body was deeply involved in each council meeting from the start. The drug nicotine stimulates the body to develop a craving not only from pure habit but also from the responses of cells and organs. The body gets a zing and strives to repeat that sensation as often as possible.

Ironically, the voice of this same body cried out danger signals as it received less of the urgently needed oxygen for the heart and other organs. Lungs cried out through the persistent cough, and arteries were no longer as open and elastic. The body itself was a divided house with a crying for more and an equally loud shout to stop!

To transform the craving, Ann began to search for new solutions to her original problem. She entertained the possibility that she just might relax without doing anything else to justify it. This required that she reconsider the message, Don't just sit there! One can, in fact, justify pure and simple relaxing. There can be such a balance between work and play, accomplishment and rest.

Ann discovered that sitting quietly with her eyes closed and breathing deeply was a way to meet many needs with no negative consequences. No voices would scold her for harmful effects upon them. If the cigarette was a friend to the earlier Ann, then a better friend was needed for the present Ann. However, the new one had to be friend to all of her.

The craver was not dealt with as an enemy to be destroyed or an alien that did not really belong to her. The craver was an Ann of earlier days who sought out the best solution she could find at that time. The craver was approached with appreciation and respect. New cooperation then became possible.

The process thus far, aided by the image of life as a series

108

of events with the Caring Friend as integral part of each, saw God as deeply involved in Ann's struggle. God was present in the council meeting in which Ann first decided to smoke. Not that this was God's vision for that moment or that God persuaded Ann toward smoking, but God was involved in Ann's search for some way to relax. A solution was found which brought relief, but it was only marginally successful then and became less so later.

The scolding voice also needed transformation. Its threats and criticisms just did not work. As long as this voice remained as an adversary to the craver, a stalemate would exist. Like two children throwing rocks at one another, they stood embattled. But then, the scolder needed to be understood, appreciated, and valued also. This was not really hard to do.

We have already seen that this voice represented the body and its experience of being suffocated, limited, and deeply harmed. The problem is not that this voice was untrue or unimportant, but rather that it had spoken in a negative way. The scolding voice was in need of transformation into a positive statement of needs. It, too, represented council meetings, some of which were in Ann's distant past.

Ann could recall the surge of energy which flowed through her as she slammed the winning spike in the state volleyball tournament, the nodding agreement she felt listening to the lecture of a respected health class teacher. She remembered the processes of a healthy body illustrated in her physiology class during nurse's training. She fully intended her vow to promote health as a registered nurse. These were more than scolders; they were events in which feelings were felt, vows were made, and values were formed.

Each scolding voice was translated into a picture of who she really wanted to become. An imaginary photo album was developed showing all the enjoyable and beneficial actions

109

she could perform and the healthy person she could be. Ann moved into images, dreams, visions, hopes, and desires—the realm where the Persuasive Presence is so uniquely involved. She began to awaken an area of her council which had been muffled before.

These pictures from the photo album included Ann jogging around the high school track, walking briskly through the shopping mall, dancing freely in the aerobics class, and hurrying from patient to nurse's station. Pictures of her body included moist, pink lungs; healthy gums; white teeth; a clear, soft complexion; and oxygen-rich blood flowing outward through her body.

Other photos included her husband's hearty congratulations and her children breathing the clean air in their home. Ann pictured herself sitting through an entire meeting without longing for a break and visiting with friends during the halftime of her son's basketball game rather than her usual hurried exit. She imagined herself as a person in control rather than being controlled. She was the decider. These pictures carried with them a flow of pride and pleasure.

Now these pictures were available to be presented at any new council meeting. This realm of possibility could become powerful rather than the heavy hand of the past dominating each meeting. Her heart's desire, the person she longed to become, the image supported by all voices could become a new voice.

One important task remained in her transformation. Ann needed to develop what she would do differently in each moment of truth—the smoking situation. Even with the best of intentions and the most vivid imagination, she could trip and fall in a difficult or trying moment. The broad images had to be translated into the tiny moment.

110

There was the first cigarette upon arising in the morning, a cigarette with breakfast, one while driving to work, one during the morning break, one or more with lunch, a cigarette with coffee after dinner, and those in the evening while reading in her favorite chair. For each of these events, it was important to have a new option ready.

Out of a number of choices, Ann thought that a small can of juice would help her cope with her first moments after awakening. Peeling, segmenting, and eating an orange would serve her well at break times. Deep breathing was a choice for Ann's tense moments. Hand lotion, slowly pressed from the tube and gently rubbed onto her hands, was the option chosen to involve her hands after dinner. Crocheting and knitting were held in reserve by her recliner chair for evening times. She chose unsalted sunflower seeds and sugarless gum to satisfy her mouth and lips during the evening. She put plastic straws cut the size of a cigarette in her purse for use during driving.

Several times each day Ann rehearsed what she would do in each of these tempting moments, just as she imagined the benefits she would gain from carrying out each new option. She might want a cigarette, but now she could readily see and feel what she wanted more than a cigarette.

The council meeting offered a way of lifting up the importance of each of these smoking events. Each was a moment of choice and each could be an accomplishment to be celebrated. Each accomplishment served to build the influence of the new ways. The tiny events were seen as of utmost importance.

Following this hard work by Ann her council meetings gradually took on a different tone than before. Instead of a meeting dominated by a powerful habit and a needful body, some new influences were now present. Images of who she might become, options of what she might do, and under-standings of her basic needs were now vivid and clear. New voices were speaking in the council.

God was present both before and now. God had been offering possibilities for health in every past event, but there was little support for them from Ann's other council members. Like a still small voice the lures of the Caring Friend were present but overwhelmed by the crushing volume of other louder voices. Now, however, there were cooperating voices increasingly emerging and rapidly growing in strength. Strength multiplied from the cooperation.

One day Ann walked right into the pictures in her photo album. She rejoiced! The Caring Friend rejoiced with her!

12.

Changing: I Can't Honestly Sing This Hymn!

THE hymn was announced from the pulpit, people began to page through their hymnals, and the organist played several introductory measures of the tune. Reaching the correct page number, Susan scanned the first verse. She was appalled. Glancing at her husband next to her in the pew, she whispered, "I can't sing this!"

The words before her were:

> There is a fountain filled with blood
> Drawn from Emmanuel's veins;
> And sinners, plunged beneath that flood,
> Lose all their guilty stains.

Rather than inspiring Susan, the image was repelling. She wondered what others were thinking about the words which the congregation had now begun to sing. Were some, like she, not singing? Were they simply mouthing the words? Or were some eagerly endorsing them? What were her children making of all this?

Susan is grappling with the world's past, one crucial member of every person's council meetings. This council member has nothing to do with her personal past, for she played no part whatsoever in the writing of this hymn. The world's past is simply given to her. That the poet William Cowper lived and wrote is fixed and completed. It is Susan who must in some way come to terms with the poet and his creation, for in this moment of worship it is fully present to her.

Susan's experience is similar to a number of worshipers today who struggle with words from the past which they are called upon to sing, affirm, confess, and pray. Susan quickly rejected this portion of the world's past. Yet the past may be also appreciated and valued.

What can be said about the world's past which so deeply enters into each person's present moments? The past is composed of events just like the present event of worship, only made up of those council members which were available at each particular stage of world history. Moreover, God was actively engaged in each of those events which flow together to form the lengthy trail behind us. All were council meetings, but the council members were different. If for no other reason than that God was present in each event, the past has some value.

Could Susan become more appreciative of this hymn? Possibly so, if by some fantasy time machine she were transported back to the world of the poet, allowing her to see the world through his eyes. She might, even then, conclude her journey by rejecting the hymn as strongly as she does now, but it would be out of a greater sense of understanding. Let us take the trip.

The journey takes us to England in the latter half of the eighteenth century, at about the time our nation was born. Obviously, the poet is referring us to the blood of Jesus as the

114

sacrifice made once for all. The fountain may well be the poet's own addition, for it is surely not a prominent symbol in the scriptures. Although he does not explain how, the poet rejoices in the transformation which can occur through the blood of Jesus—from guilt to freedom, from stain to purity. Susan could hear him proclaiming meaning and joy in his day.

To fully understand the hymn, however, our journey must penetrate farther into the past to the time of Jesus. In this era is to be found the more complete meaning of the healing blood. Susan could stand among those who searched for ways to speak about the life, death, and resurrection of Jesus in a way which would express the astounding new life they had experienced. One powerful image they found was comparing Jesus to the ritual of sacrifice. What is Jesus like? He is like the lamb sacrificed for a sin offering. He is like the high priest who makes the sacrifice for all the community, not yearly, but once for all.

To compare Jesus to the sacrifice required that this ritual be widely known and, indeed, it was. It had been a part of their daily lives for generations prior to Jesus' birth. Since it was so familiar it became a most convincing way to talk about the new event—the Christ event. Thus, we are led on our journey even farther into the past in order to appreciate that to which Jesus was compared.

To understand the hymn in its depth we must take part in the Jewish community prior to Jesus. Susan could accompany a person who had sinned and is now entering the temple to be cleansed of that sin. Buying a pigeon or dove from one of the many vendors in the courtyard, the sinner enters the temple and presents the animal to the priest. The priest sacrifices the animal on the altar. Blood flows. Dipping his finger into the blood on the altar, the priest daubs a tiny touch of blood at three places on the sinner's right side—ear, thumb, and large toe. Both sinner and priest believe that this particular act will transform the person from sin to wholeness. Blood has a restoring power. Blood is a vital force.

After completing this ritual, the person feels free and whole in contrast to the earlier divided and distorted self. The person's relationship with God has been restored. Walking away from the altar and out of the temple with that person, Susan could rejoice with one who now feels new. She could feel with that person. She need not hold the same beliefs about the transforming power of blood in order to join in the rejoicing.

Somewhere, sometime in the deeper recesses of antiquity there must have been events in which the idea that blood is healing was first discovered and gradually became effective. Those vague events, however, are beyond Susan's itinerary. They remain unclear. However, some things are now clear to Susan. Early Christians proclaimed that what Jesus had done for them was like that which the sacrifice had accomplished. They felt free, transformed, whole, and restored with God, just as when they had left the temple. Furthermore, they exclaimed that, in contrast to the animal rituals, this sacrifice need never be offered again.

In the journey, Susan could feel with and rejoice with those who lived during the different layers of history: the Jew leaving the temple, the Christian following the resurrection, and the eighteenth-century poet imagining a fountain. She may not use the same words today, she may not hold the same beliefs today; yet she can appreciate their responses of freedom, newness, aliveness, and wholeness. With those experiences she can identify.

Following the journey, we may be curious about whether Susan might be more open to sing praises in the words of the poet, the Christian, the Jew. They are not her words. They are, rather, voices of the past, speaking in the present. Even if unwilling to do so, out of a sense of conscience or a need to use modern language, at least she may be more appreciative of the praises from the past.

We may struggle with Susan about whether or not to allow William Cowper's "There Is a Fountain Filled with Blood" to be a part of our tradition. We may ask ourselves how much of the total past we will include as our past. It is possible to imagine our past as a vast funnel sweeping out in an ever-increasing arc inlcuding more and more of the experiences of Christian tradition, Jewish tradition, human tradition, natural history, and inorganic history.

Just as each yearly Passover feast is begun by reciting "A wandering Aramean was my father" (Deut. 26:5), so we may want to enrich our personal past by including a multitude of historical events as the activity of our own mothers and fathers. Frequently we reject that tradition which does not speak in precisely the words which we employ today. How enriched our present worship would be if we chose to celebrate not only in the modern ways but also in the words of those who have lived before us.

How much more we would appreciate the meaning of creation if we sang and danced with the small band of Hebrew slaves just saved from the pursuing Egyptian soldiers and even now being formed into a people! How much more deeply we would affirm the Nicene Creed if we entered into the city of Nicaea in A.D. 325 with the bishops, pondering with them how to express both the divine experience and the human experience in Jesus.

How much more joyfully we would sing "A Mighty Fortress Is Our God" if we walked into the feudal world of Martin Luther! How much more authentically we would approach the Holy Communion chalice and receive the words "The blood of Christ shed for thee" if we walked to the temple altar with the Jewish sinner.

While there is great need to create worship which speaks in the language of our day, it is also important that we feel with those who have gone before, those who have left behind their understanding of the good news in their words from their day. The lure is that we feel with persons of the past and invite them to become a part of our past.

13.

Puzzled:
The Way I Was Raised
Isn't Working with My Kids

*I*T seemed to Marge that she was working harder than her daughter, Jan. Each school night she would ask Jan if she had any homework and would often sit for hours assisting her with class assignments. Marge wanted her daughter to do well in the eighth grade. The fleeting glances Jan would steal from the book on the kitchen table to the television in the family room made Marge wonder which of them was learning business math.

Homework was not the whole story. The stress of nagging had finally caused Marge to throw up her hands and stop telling Jan to make her bed each morning. In giving up, Marge felt that she had failed to instill neatness and self-discipline in her daughter. Her requirement that Jan wear a dress to school once a week was fast coming to a head, for she had heard that Jan was changing into jeans before her first-period class. She knew that she had to confront Jan soon but was dreading the fireworks. Grounding her for the weekend had not worked with the messy room, and Marge had no hope that it would work here either. She was running out of threats.

Shopping was losing its enjoyment. Jan was continually pulling at Marge's coat sleeve to look at the latest designer jeans or name-brand blouse. Whenever Marge grew weary of saying no, she was nickeled and dimed to death. Although each of the three children was assigned certain chores, there was always some reason why Jan could not do the dishes on her night. Reasons soon deteriorated into harsh words and arguments. Even with Jan in her room crying after an angry exit, the dinner dishes remained in the sink. At times it seemed easier for Marge to do the task herself than to work out all of Jan's carefully planned resistance.

Marge was really bothered that Jan's many promises made to persuade them to buy the puppy she wanted so badly were not being kept. There were many mornings when Buffy was not fed and her water dish was dry, while the neatly typed rules for caring for the puppy hung prominently nearby on the refrigerator door.

Taxi service was a constant battle. After eight hours at the insurance office, Marge was ready to prop up her feet for a few quiet moments with the newspaper before starting dinner. In those same moments, Jan, who had been home for nearly two hours, often unveiled an immediate need to be taken somewhere. The need might be to buy brown and gold socks she needed for the next day's drill team performance, to take the friend home who had stayed to do a project with Jan, or to get the brownie mix necesssary for the bake sale. Marge sensed in those moments that Jan knew that her mother would give in. Even after putting her foot down several weeks ago—Wednesdays and weekends only for chauffeuring—Marge knew that she was defeated and would not carry out her own demands. She was trapped, because she did want her daughter to have the enriching experiences and friendships of the junior high years.

Marge is not that different from many working mothers with teenage daughters. All relationships have their strains and tensions, yet love still prevails. Nevertheless, she was asking herself some hard questions as a parent. Should I be having such angry feelings with my daughter? Should I be ending up so critical of myself? Why can't it go better between us?

As she looked back at her own childhood, she didn't see all these problems. Her folks set down rules and she obeyed them. While it was not always easy for her and she never told her parents everything, they got along well. But when she tried to use the same methods with her daughter, they didn't work. She wondered what was lacking in her that she hadn't been able to do what her parents did. She wondered what was wrong with her daughter that she couldn't just mind.

In Marge's inner struggle, would it make any difference if she had a new vision of God? The answer offered here is a hearty Yes! Being related to a God who feels everything one feels and who speaks with persuasion can make a world of difference in personal relationships.

At present Marge is caught up in the need for control, which has developed into a subtle, and sometimes explosive, power struggle. Often this approach reflects a God of power. This God is like the top of a chain of command—husband obeys God, wife obeys husband, and children obey mother. Who's in charge here is amply clear. Marge was probably raised by parents who held this image of God. She remembered clearly, If you put your feet under my table, you follow my rules!

Those parenting in this style usually think and talk in the following words: rules . . . tell . . . have to . . . threat

. . . make you . . . mind . . . obey . . . rebel . . . rewards . . . punishment. Power is something that is limited in quantity—the more one has, the less the other has. If the parent does not keep control, the child will take over. Someone must be in control; someone has the power.

The council meeting portrays a picture of persuasive power. God is present, but not as the one in command. God persuades but does not make, influences but does not force. God creates with persons and desires the increase of the person's creative power. Each new possibility which God offers becomes part of the discussion in the council, not an order. A parenting style grounded here is based on the affirmation that if God is empathic and persuasive with parents, they may risk being so with their children.

This vision of God prompts thinking and talking in new words: problems . . . conflicts . . . sharing . . . listening . . . confronting . . . consulting . . . negotiating . . . deciding . . . agreements . . . contracts . . . consequences. Rather than power struggles which focus upon mother versus daughter as separate and distinct wills, this new vision promotes a mother taking into account both herself and her daughter and a daughter considering the needs of both herself and her mother.

Having set the stage, let us see how Marge's approach might be changed if she took the image of council meeting seriously. We can watch for her listening, sharing, and negotiating, much like the voice of a persuasive member of the council.

Marge decided to talk with Jan, and especially to listen to her, to see if they could really understand one another. She intentionally began with one of the easier problems—making the bed.

"For the life of me, I don't understand why it's such a big deal to make your bed each morning. I do it myself. It takes less than five minutes."

"Mom, you don't get it. It isn't the time. I just don't want to make my bed."

"But why?"

"I don't see any sense in it. It's just not important to me."

"But what about learning habits of neatness?"

"I already know I can be neat. I learned that in the fourth grade. Remember? So, I can do it, so what?"

"Jan, now be honest with me. Don't you deep down want some order in your life?"

"Wait a minute, Mom. I have order in my life without making my bed! Nobody sees it anyhow, except maybe you and Dad and Brad. Why does it matter to you?"

"Well . . . I guess I never thought it mattered so much to me. I thought I was doing something for you."

"Gosh, it's never been much of a problem to me, except your harping on it all the time. Why is it so important to you? Why do you make such a big deal out of it?"

"OK . . . let me think a minute. I suppose it's that I want to know that I've been a good mother to you and taught you good habits you will use the rest of your life. And . . . I know how embarrassed I was when my friends had to walk by your room to put their coats on our bed."

"Mom, I don't think I have to make my bed every day for you to be a good mother. You've taught me lots of good things. I watch you more than you think. I know how to be tidy when I want to be. I've learned. The clothes I wear are neat. I'm

123

always on time to school. Making my bed just isn't a place I need to be tidy."

"You mean I've been pushing you to do what I think is important and you don't?"

"Right!"

"OK, OK, I see. You are really fine with a bed that's not made?"

"That's right."

"I still have a feeling I would be letting you down by not making you be disciplined."

"All I do is dig my heels in deeper when you push!"

"So we reach a stand-off. Nobody wins."

"That's for sure."

"So, I wonder what we can do to stop our fighting and keep us both OK?"

"Well . . . how about each week when you wash the sheets, I'll make my bed that day?"

"Leave it unmade the rest of the week?"

"Yeah."

"I guess I could live with that. Maybe I could close your door if it really gets to me. . . . But what about when guests come?"

"Close the door anytime you want."

"All right, but my friends . . ."

"Hmmm . . . what about you leaving me a note the night

124

before on the bathroom mirror, and I'll make my bed that day?"

"Well, I guess that would help my embarrassment."

Neither Marge nor Jan employed the best in sharing and listening skills, but each one made a good start. They had made agreements based on trying to understand one another. The experiment was now on. More important than the contract was the spirit of cooperation which was interwoven with the negotiating.

Once gaining some confidence in her first talk with Jan, Marge moved on to the more troubling issue, one about which both harbored stronger feelings. Getting up her nerve for the encounter, Marge engaged her daughter on homework.

"Jan, we've got to get something worked out about your homework."

"Aw, Mom, why spoil a perfectly good evening talking about that stuff?"

"I know, I know. I don't want to get into it either, but I'm going out of my mind with what's happening now."

"All right, but I want to watch something on TV at eight."

"Now, let's try to reason with each other. Let's keep the lid on our feelings and talk civilized to each other."

"I hope we can."

"Let's each start by talking about the problem. No one interrupts until both of us have had our say. You can go first if you want to."

"No, you brought it up. You go first."

"OK, here's how it is with me. I'm at my wit's end with sitting every night in the kitchen with you over those books! I've just had it! I . . ."

"Well, it was your idea to—"

"Whoa! Remember? No one interrupts. Do you want to go first?"

"No, you go on. Let's get on with it."

"All I want is the best for you. I give up my evenings after I work all day so that you can do your best in school. What do I get for it? A lot of static. You sit and doodle or you're staring off in space daydreaming about something. If not that, you're sneaking glances at the TV. I give up my time for you and you want me to do your work. I'm tired of working harder than you do. I've got two other kids to look after. I sacrifice for you and do I get any appreciation? Hardly, you seem to resent me for it. I'm—"

"C'mon, Mom, not another lecture! I've gotta say something."

"But the rule. No interrupting."

"That's just it! You always make up the rules. Rules, rules, rules! Everywhere I walk in this house there are your little rules. How about me making the rules for a change?"

"Young lady, my father would have had you over his knee by now if you were his kid!"

"So, I could be so lucky!"

"OK . . . Now wait a minute. . . . Let's cool off. . . . There, let's start a different way. We need to talk and get some things

126

worked out. Now, I really want to hear how you see all this. Why don't you go ahead and have your say?"

"You won't interrupt me?"

"No, I won't."

"OK then, here's how it is. You've got me trapped. I either lie or sit in that dumb kitchen with you. Do you want me to lie? Sure, I could say, 'No, Mom, no homework tonight.' Then when you get the poor work slip from school I've had it. You've got me coming and going. So what's wrong with stealing a little fun in a boring, boring, boring evening? You even said that TV's out till I get it all done. That's like never, so good-bye TV. And what's more, maybe I don't want to do my best. You keep nagging me, 'Do your best, do your best.' What about what I want? I don't know if I'm turned off by school or your nagging. You just don't trust me. Did it ever occur to you that maybe I could figure out when to study? Maybe I can make up my own mind about what grade I want? Wendy's folks don't bug her about her homework, and she gets good grades. Huh, all I hear is 'better get those A's and B's if you want to go to activity night . . . or spend the night with Cathy . . . or get that driver's license someday.' I get sick of it. . . . Well, I guess that's it."

"Wow, that's a bundle!"

"Right!"

"Now I'm going to try my level best to take all that in. So you're trapped. And here I thought *I* was the one who was trapped."

"I don't have any say in it."

"You feel that I have all the say. I make all the rules."

"Exactly!"

"You think that you should decide when you study and what grades you'll try for."

"Why not? I'm a teenager now."

"You think that we hold threats over your head about grades."

"Yeah, and it sure feels like you and Dad don't trust me. You treat me like a baby."

"I think I'm getting the picture. Now, let me tell you what I want for you. Will you listen, just for a minute?"

"Sure, OK."

"I want good things for you. Life is hard, and I want you to have a good start on it. I want you to know how to study. I want you to have a good education, a good job someday. You know I didn't finish school, and I've had some deep regrets about that. I want it better for you than I've had it. If it seems like pushing and nagging, it's been for your own good. I'm sorry I didn't listen more to my folks. You've got a good mind, and I want you to use it. I want to be proud of you."

"I know that, Mom. I know you want the best for me."

"I'm glad you do—"

"But why not let me figure it out for myself? Who knows, I might even get good grades on my own!"

"That would sure be nice. But if I leave you on your own, will you just goof around? I've sure seen you do a lot of that in the kitchen. What'll you do without those rules?"

"Well, maybe I'd go for an A in art, but a C in history."

"Shouldn't you be doing your best in everything?"

"Maybe so, but I'd like to find out what I really like. You hear, what *I* like! I'm not going to flunk out, Mom."

"So, what if I didn't work with you on your homework? Would you get it done? Would you ask me when you really need my help?"

"Wow, that would be a relief! I'd get it done my own way. I might watch a little TV, then go to my room. I might get more done in prep period."

"You say that now, but would you follow through?"

"That's just it—you never trust me! What do I have to do?"

"Oops, sorry. I really do want to trust you. It's just so different. Well, how about a limited time offer?"

"What's that?"

"You know, like the offers on TV. We might try it for awhile. What if I didn't ask you about homework and you would ask me when you needed help?"

"That might work OK. You really wouldn't bug me?"

"I know that I might have to bite my tongue sometimes, but I'd sure try."

"Maybe I'd even want to tell you about what I'm doing in school."

"That would be nice. And it sure would be a relief for me to have some evenings to do some other things. I hope you know it's no fun to be a nag."

"What if they send home a poor work slip?"

"I'd be mighty edgy about it. I might slip a little myself—into my old ways. What I hope I'd say is, 'Jan, what do you plan to do about this?' and 'Jan, remember that if you need my help, I'm here.' "

"That would sound really good. This has really helped. I think I feel better."

Marge and Jan had broken the barrier of rules and rebellion. While there were many more hurdles to encounter, they had begun an adventure of a persuasive relationship—one which is at the very heart of the universe.

14.

Ignoring: It's Too Scary to Think About

WHERE is God when we think the unthinkable? Where is God present in the events which could lead to nuclear holocaust? While it seems more comforting simply to ignore the question, to do so indefinitely is impossible.

Let us look briefly at the ways three persons would answer the questions, then see how viewing life in terms of council meetings offers a different answer. We begin with the facts that most persons, even children, know today. There could be a nuclear accident or nuclear war with the most devastating effects for all of life. The pictures of such a disaster have been painted vividly. Given these facts, we turn to interpretation. Where is God in the midst of these disastrous possibilities?

Sandy answers this question easily. God won't let it happen. Like a mother watching her child play in the yard, who swoops down upon him when he ventures too near the street, so God may allow us to reach the brink but will not allow us to fall over the cliff. The creation is much too precious for God to allow rebellious children to destroy it.

Moreover, God has all of the power necessary to prevent such destruction. Just as God intervened during many crises in the Bible, so God can act again. As the hymn writer proclaims, "This Is My Father's World." Sandy would urge everyone to place their trust in the Almighty God of creation.

Mel would agree with Sandy, except he would add more. Not only is God in control, but the future is set also. God knows it all from start to finish, and God will be a part of the finish. The very crises which frighten most people cause Mel to rejoice because they are the signs of the end of time bringing with it the second coming of Christ. Each war and rumor of war are heralded as a step toward the final battle between God and evil—Armageddon.

Certainly one does not want to see creation destroyed, but the greater riches to be gained by its destruction makes them incomparable to the present world. The old will give way to the unbelievably wondrous new. God has announced how the future will unfold in the Bible for all to hear. Mel would call others to be certain that they are righteous so that when Christ returns they will be gathered up with the saints in glory.

Carl would have none of that which Sandy and Mel believe. As a humanist he would say that the responsibility for the future of the world is in our hands and our hands alone. He would judge the believers who think that God will bail us out when the going gets tough as escapists. If there is no God in the universe, then surely there can be no help from that source.

While Carl puts much thought and energy into working to prevent a nuclear holocast, he is aware of other humanists who escape as much as Christians. There are those who say that since the disaster may happen at any moment it is good to live to the fullest now. Waiting, disciplining, and depriving have no place in their agenda. Still others may experi-

132

ence great fear and anxiety about the possible sudden ending of all of life. While Carl has felt all of their feelings, he has found a balance of concern, work, and pleasure. Humanity has progressed to this point by using its own resources, and the nuclear problem can be faced also.

Joyce differs from the others by affirming a persuasive God. She shares the concern and worry of Carl, but she feels that she has resources besides her own to rely upon. She shares the belief in God with Sandy and Mel, but not the God who decides when to intervene and not the God who has the future all mapped out. By understanding the events of her life as the results of council meetings, Joyce comes to some different conclusions about the nuclear threat.

God is truly persuasive. This means that God does not control the outcome of decisions made in life. It does not mean that God allows some decisions and not others. It does not mean that God will decide to step in here but not there. A primary quality of God is that of loving persuasion. Power which controls is not present. A new understanding of power is necessary. The primary power is to influence the person. Consequently, if some crazed, enraged, or desperate person were to press the doomsday button, God could not stop the act. Influence, yes; stop, no!

At this point, the role of God in any event is not fully comforting. We cannot simply ignore the threat and know that God will do what is best for us. We are the deciders. God is our influencer. It is doubtful that we want to carry that responsibility, but it is nonetheless ours. We cannot have God be persuader when we want it so and have God as controller when it is convenient for us.

Joyce also takes seriously the notion that if God acts as persuader in each council meeting, then the future is not yet known. In this sense there is no member of the council who knows what will happen until the meeting is over. No one comes into the meeting with the knowledge of the outcome. Future becomes potential. Future is possibilities. Future is as yet unknown to all.

God is the member most likely to know the possibilities simply because God is intimately involved with the council meetings of all other persons and living creatures in the world. Still, even that is not to know what Joyce will decide in the next moment. In this manner, she will see the wars and rumors of wars much differently than Mel. If there is no fixed future known only by God toward which all creation moves, then there cannot be signs which herald such a future.

Joyce cannot merely turn over the nuclear threat, as Sandy does, to God, who will stop it before it gets out of hand; nor can she applaud the signs of the approaching Armageddon with Mel. She cannot join with either of them. On the other hand, she cannot agree with Carl that the only resources in coping with the threat are human. Joyce finds a different path which wends its way near theirs but is not theirs.

Joyce's hope is the affirmation that God is luring all creation toward love, beauty, and harmony. Such is the basic nature of God. There is no need to wonder what God desires in basic outline for life on earth. Nor is there need to wonder if God desires utter destruction of life. With this luring voice in every council meeting of every person on earth, there is truly a resource which is beyond the human. To listen to this voice is to be in harmony with the deepest and most pervasive Love of the universe.

Nevertheless, God is often thwarted. The desire for beauty is often smashed into the ugly and distorted. There is surely no guarantee that the beautiful will emerge and prevail. Much evidence points in the other direction. Still,

134

beauty is the tender lure offered by God in each event in every locale. The call for Joyce and others is to cooperate with this desire for the beautiful. It is for this cooperation that she and all of us are responsible. In this sense she joins with Carl.

An even deeper resource is available to Joyce and to all who affirm a lovingly persuasive God. This is that God saves each event which occurs in one's life. Each act, however small, which promotes peace and harmony is saved everlastingly in God's own being. While Carl may have to succeed in his venture to feel successful, Joyce need only carry out one small act after another to feel the meaning in her efforts.

Joyce knows that there is no guarantee that a nuclear holocaust will be prevented. Living out of an image of council meetings carries with it that somber note. There is joy in affirming her Caring Friend and her freedom to choose, but there is also the realism of possible disaster.

What would such a disaster look like for persons and for God? God would feel the impact in just the same manner as all living things. The stabbing shock of those instantly annihilated and the enduring suffering of those who survived the initial destruction would be felt equally by God. The Caring One, who is part of every council meeting, would experience everything right along with the total council.

Those unspeakably tearing moments would be saved, along with all those that went before, in the life of God. All of the events of a life up to that instant would be gathered up. Nothing would be lost.

To whomever and whatever survived, God would offer the next lure to move forward. Loving possibilities would come forth from God. Some estimate that the survivors may be the insects, like the tiny marsupials who inherited the earth from the dinosaurs. If that be, then they will be the ones with whom God will create the next stage of life on earth.

We are the ones who have much to say about which direction our planet will take. We hold the destiny of the helpless in our hands—the children, the animals, and the plants. Yet we are not alone nor are we the only ones who care. With the One who actively participates in every council meeting, we are co-creators of life.

15.

Dying: What Do I Write to Aunt Vera?

MY wife's aunt knew that she was dying. She had questions. What was it like ahead? Was there something to hope for? Did her life add up to something significant? Even though she had not been active in the church recently, did God still care for her? Her concern prompted my letter to Vera.

Monday, January 31

Dear Vera,

Aneyth called yesterday to tell us of your days together and the difficult decision you faced about whether or not to have the radiation therapy with the hospitalization. I am sure it was hard to know what was best for you, and we all wish you well in carrying out your decision.

We surely feel for you with the losses you have been facing. Life must have little taste left in it—little to look forward to when talking is so tiring, energy is so limited, and food offers little pleasure. We send our blessings in the midst of all that loss.

I do want to share with you some thoughts I have about the meaning of all this, hoping that you will find it of some comfort and hope to you.

As I see you, you have lived with a sense of joy, pleasure, and humor—with gusto. I recall your diamond-laden fingers on your eightieth birthday celebration. To the way you have chosen to live, I say bravo! You have provided each of us with a model which is worthy of emulating.

What I want to share is the hope that I see even now in the midst of your losses. First, I know God to be a fellow adventurer, going with us wherever we go. God has been a part of and surely enjoyed the gusto with which you have met life.

God is equally present in any losses. In fact, I think that God feels each feeling, experiences each event in precisely and exactly the same way that we do—joy when we rejoice, agony when we agonize.

There is no depth of feeling, no thought which God does not have right along with us. God not only understands us but truly feels with us whatever we face and endure. The word we hear from scripture, "Lo, I am with you always . . ." is true. We haven't always known about a suffering God, a celebrating God, a hurting God, an agonizing God, but so God is.

Second, I see God as one who is always calling us forward into the next event, calling us to some new experience, new growth, new wholeness. It is only because God feels precisely what we feel, knows us intimately from within, that God can offer us just that right call or possibility which fits the need of our next moment. God always uses persuasion, influence, luring, calling—never force or coercion or power. This is part and parcel of God's graceful love to us.

So I will share the confidence that in your present

experiences God is present feeling with you and luring you on to the next step to be taken.

Third, I want to share that no event or experience in our lives is ever lost. Each is saved and taken up to enrich God's life. Whether the event was twenty minutes ago or fifty years ago, that event is clear and vivid in God's expansive vision. This means that your moments and mine have eternal value, they are saved forever. Each moment of our lives as it concludes finds a home with God and is woven into the beautiful complex fabric which is God's life.

Fourth, I want to say that, thereby, our total lives are not lost either. Because each event is saved, so is the total stream of events which compose our lives. Our person, our personality, our self is too precious to be lost, so we are saved. Even death cannot cause the loss.

I have come to call the event of death the next adventure. Not the end, not a loss or waste of all that has grown and developed, but a moving into a new relation with God which has already been occurring here.

I see the next adventure as one where we are transformed gradually so that we can be related and connected with everything with God as the great web, or the glue, or the symphony that ties all the notes together.

I think we will continue to grow in love, caring, and giving as we are beautifully related to all persons who have ever lived as well as all that has occurred in nature. That we would see loved ones again in the next adventure is accurate, but too narrow—not rich and full enough. I affirm Paul the apostle when he says that nothing can separate us from the love of God in Christ.

I see each of us being changed and transformed into the fully blossomed flower which we can be, obtaining much of our beauty from the vast array of other flowers in the garden.

Life beyond this life is adventure, more exciting and fulfilling than we have known here.

These are hopes and images that I affirm, and I offer them to you. I hope that they enrich those to which you already hold.

You have a great spirit! You have embraced and squeezed life heartily, for which I applaud you. I am sure that God has laughed with you and has cried with you and is ever with you.

With our caring love and with the Grace and Peace of God.

Bob and Adrienne

16.

Adjusting: Praying through the Snowstorm

THE plan was all set. It had been for a month. Thursday I would take the early flight from Wenatchee to Seattle, lead the one-day seminar, and be on a plane for Claremont, California, by early evening. I had even made arrangements to drive my car in the event that our tiny airport closed because of fog, a fairly frequent happening in winter. The studded tires were on and the gas tank was full.

Friends would meet me at the airport in California; I would engage in committee work with my colleagues, share and laugh with them over dinner the next evening, visit with my student friends at the seminary, then cap off the trip with an overnight stay with my daughter and son-in-law. All this and be home in time for work Monday morning was the design. The tiny snowflake changed it all. To adjust to these changes required praying constantly (from 1 Thess. 5:7).

The flight to Seattle was uneventful; the entire scenery below us was the cloud cover. For the first time I saw Seattle as white squares of neighborhoods outlined by black streets, the remains of the recent and most unusual snowstorm.

Traffic moved quickly at 6:45 A.M. as my friend Norm drove me from the Seattle-Tacoma airport to his suburban home where the seminar was to be held. Over breakfast we watched the first flakes of snow fall. Little did we know how many more would follow that day. We were given our first vivid clue when three of the group arrived over one and one-half hours late from a normally easy drive from downtown Seattle. Roads were slick, drivers were inexperienced with snow, and few had snow tires. The first of many changes occurred when we had to begin the seminar late. The changes would magnify as we became aware of our snow-bound condition.

In what way did my understanding of the council meeting affect my feelings and decisions in this rapidly changing situation? How did I pray to God to ask for directions?

There were several ideas about praying to God which I did not entertain. I did not see the snowstorm as an act of an almighty God who controls the fall of every tiny snowflake. In this way I did not have to search for God's lesson for me or ask how this storm fits into God's preordained plan for my life. Nor did I see any divine plan to punish us or thwart what we wanted to accomplish. Likewise, there was no need in any moment to ask God to be present with us, for I had the strongest sense that God was fully present in everyone.

In my council meetings of the next two days the following prayer in its several forms served as my guide:

O God of Grace,
May I be aware of your highest possibility for this moment, and may I be willing to act upon it.
O Christ,
May I be open to your transforming power as I enter this new event.

142

O God,
May I capture a glimpse of your harmonious vision for this moment now forming.
O Great Adventurer of the Universe,
What is the loving act needed in this situation?
Gracious God,
Illumine my awareness in this situation with the shining ray of your desire for this occasion.

The first of many council meetings was held as the day progressed and the snow outside the window piled up. We had already eaten lunch at Norm's home rather than at the expected restaurant. With road conditions worsening, it was becoming increasingly clear that there just may not be time to reach the airport for my next flight. It was suggested that I might leave early.

My council had already been in session quietly weighing this question and now I faced it openly. Naturally, some voices spoke for the desire to leave early, relax after a hard week, and keep on schedule. Others brought out that my first responsibility was to the seminar group. I asked that I might be aware of God's most loving vision for me in this moment. Answers began to form. Only I could effectively lead a seminar which I had designed, while I was only one of a dozen on the committee at Claremont. They could function without me. The council decision was clear: I would stay the allotted time, leaving open what to do next.

The decision was clear but not without loss. I did not like to lose my picture of a leisurely dinner at thirty thousand feet, watching the red sky to the west. Nor did I like the uncertainty of not knowing what I would do next. I decided to focus upon the seminar and simply say that I do not know yet what I will do after it is over. For a former Boy Scout who still believes in the motto "Be Prepared," this was most difficult.

What I thought would be a difficult council meeting at the conclusion of the seminar was actually quite easy. The Seattle-Tacoma airport was closed due to the heavy snowfall, and no flights were arriving or departing. That was settled, but now what was God's loving possibility for this new moment?

People were putting on overshoes, coats, and scarves and brushing off eight inches of new snow from their cars. After some farewell remarks, the next step became quite clear. "Change into your older clothes and help friends put chains on their car." While some huddled around the television watching for the latest report on road conditions, we were jacking up the car and working with the seldom-used chains. Soon they left in a flurry.

There was nothing for me to do except spend the night. An earlier council meeting had ruled out asking my friend Norm to take me to the airport, where I would simply wait for the next southbound plane. I could not ask that of him, not knowing what we would find on the highways. And the television reports of the hundreds of travelers stranded at the airport did not look appealing.

Norm's wife, Lola, and her mother, Ila, began to prepare dinner. What is the loving act for this moment? My council had little difficulty in deciding. "Stir the waffle batter."

Dinner finished and the dishes placed in the dishwasher, my council faced a new moment. This one seemed easy. Norm was outside with the snowblower. I grabbed coat, gloves, and a snowshovel and joined him. Inside again I reflected on the many facets of my council: the continuing snowfall, the closed airport, the treacherous roads, the loaded telephone circuits, my desire to hold onto my earlier plans, my tired body which had arisen at 4:30 that morning, the needs of my friends where I was staying, my wife at home, and my friends in Claremont. I groped for my next move. What was the loving response to this situation?

It became clear that I needed to be responsible to my friends in Claremont. I could not allow them to make a twenty-minute drive to the Ontario airport only to find that no flight was to arrive from Seattle. After a number of busy signals, I reached them and described my plight of many unknowns.

My friend Judy was most gracious. She would tell the committee of my situation so that they too would not be wondering about my absence. As I shared words with her, I became more deeply aware of my loss at not winging my way to California and greeting friends with handshake and embrace, meeting new people, engaging in stimulating discussions, catching up on the latest events, asking my planned questions, and savoring the mild temperatures of a lovely evening. I felt that I was making caring decisions, but I hurt!

The next moment unfolded easily. I needed to tell my wife, Adrienne, of my situation and share that I would not know until the next day whether I would be speaking to her from California, Seattle, or home. Her understanding and caring helped soothe the hurt. I was grateful. My bases were covered for the moment.

Although my body was tired and my mind foggy, the next loving act seemed amply clear. I would share in the game my friend loves so well. Bruce, Norm, and I sat down to a game of three-handed pinochle, then watched the 11:00 weather reports.

Luckily, I was able to sleep even in the midst of many unknowns. I fell into bed, shared my gratefulness to God for an honest and meaningful seminar and a safe and warm place to lay my head, and quickly drifted into sleep.

I awoke very nervous. I did not know what I would do. I needed to hear the weather reports and the road conditions. After a quick shower, I heard from the radio report that all schools were closed, but planes were flying once again. Efforts to telephone were utterly thwarted. I could not reach the airlines, the depot, or Amtrak railroad. Obviously, I was not the only one checking out options.

This was the toughest council meeting of all. Should I try to make it to Claremont with less than a day of the two-day meeting remaining or should I simply find a way back home? I consulted my council members. The most powerful member was the world about me—the weather conditions. While a clearing was present now, a second storm was expected the day before I was to return from California. Surely, if I went to the airport I could find some flight, but was less than a day of meeting and visits with friends and my daughter worth the possibility of being stranded in Clare-mont, Portland, or Seattle on my return?

A second vocal council member was my body. I was stressed and tired. In the last five days I had made four presentations, the seminar being the last. Could I handle the fast-moving pace of California, the few hours of sleep each night, and the unknown weather situation on my return?

"O God, what is your loving possibility for me in this moment?" I received mixed messages as I listened to the council. I strongly wished that someone else would decide for me. Please, tell me what to do! I will feel regret and loss if I turn back and fear and stress if I go forward. Regret would be doubly strong if I turned back and later found that the second storm would not have hampered my return. This council meeting was truly divided. I could not fully win either way.

I sensed a strong urge to take care of myself. My body won. I would head home. I reached Amtrak and surprisingly they had a reservation for later that afternoon. I would feel

loss, but now I could experience one of my heartfelt desires—
I could travel over the Cascade Mountains on a lovely moon-
lit night through evergreens laden with snow. It was a nice
reward for my loss. I called Claremont to tell them not to
expect me and Adrienne to ask her to meet the evening
train. Now, what of the next moment?

Bruce, who had spent the night also, was preparing to
leave, and it seemed natural to help prepare his car for the
trip. A short time later we had brushed the snow off, scraped
the windows, and fitted chains on the tires.

The day began to form up for us. There were groceries to
be bought, for most were used by the unexpected lunch
guests and the two extra for dinner and breakfast. Moreover,
an open house was scheduled for the next day. I wondered
how I might help to enrich this day. It required little thought
and certainly no resistance in the council to decide to offer
to take my friends to lunch in a quaint shopping village
nearby after we shopped for groceries. The only requirement
left was for Norm to drive me to the downtown Seattle
Amtrak station later in the afternoon. This day was forming
up nicely indeed! Time with friends, a pleasant lunch, then
a relaxing ride on the train. I could relax now and let it
unfold.

I settled back with a magazine for a few moments in the
family room. My few belongings were packed, my bed made,
and I was ready. This day looked fun, and the next two days
held the bonus of being at home with nothing scheduled.

Suddenly I was brought to an unexpected decision.
Clint was at the door ready to drive back to Wenatchee.
Having forgotten some items from the day before, he stopped
by to get them. My council meeting was a mob scene. What
better opportunity could I want? But what about my pleasant
day and the fun train ride? I asked for a few minutes to pull
my thoughts together. "O Gracious One, what is the most

loving act for this situation?" I had made too many decisions in the last twenty-four hours. I didn't want to face another one. I had thought everything was all settled. Yet the world was present, calling for my choice.

I tried to hear each council member. I was looking forward to the train ride as a real treat. But to do so required that Norm take me into Seattle. I knew he would be glad to do so; however, if he didn't have to do so, he could spend the time preparing for the open house or doing some needed task. Possibly, he could even take a well-earned nap.

What about Lola and Ila? I knew that they would enjoy our time together, but they too faced major responsibilities for their next day's open house. And how would Clint feel? Would he feel some rejection if I did not accept his offer to share the ride? Surely, he would face a three-hour drive alone if I did not go. I could enjoy good conversation with a friend. Then I could be home by mid-afternoon rather than early evening.

I was aware that I could easily go either way. The council weighed the advantages of Norm not having to drive into Seattle, the company and potential help I would offer to Clint on the drive home, and the savings in money and time I would make. I gathered my things, said my farewells, and climbed into the car.

As we drove through the winter wonderland of white mountains graced with tall frosted evergreens bordered by blue skies and illumined by bright sunshine, I wondered if anything could be more beautiful. I loved it. Still, I was aware of the varied losses I was experiencing by my many decisions of these last twenty-four hours. There was real regret at not seeing my friends and my daughter in California. I questioned whether I should have given up my fun train ride. I wondered how I would feel if that second storm never reached Seattle with force and I could have arrived home again safely and on schedule.

There was a tinge of guilt that I may have played it safe and not taken the more enriching way. On the other hand, I knew the helpless feeling of being stranded and the distress of missing my first day back at work.

I ask God to help me to accept the decisions that I have made in each unfolding council meeting and to know that any one moment cannot fulfill all desires. I need help in focusing on what this next moment holds in terms of loving and beautiful possibilities. I do not require that the decisions that I reached are the "right" ones. I want only to live each moment in its fullness without ever knowing the degree to which a different choice might have led me to possibilities more fulfilling to me and to others around me.

Above all, O God, lure me to continue to desire to be aware of your vision for the new moment, then boldly make my decision. Lure me to keep risking and adventuring with you.

17.

Adventuring: On with the Show!

*I*T is time for me to encourage you in your own adventure, and I will start with a few words of summary. I have presented an image of God and shown how this image affects my life. I think of God as constantly present with me, not as one who intervenes once in a while. I may feel alone, but I do not think of myself as alone. I know God is in the tiny and ordinary events of my daily living, not just the major crossroads. I experience God as persuasive, not controlling.

I am aware of God's desire for me to become graceful, harmonious, and beautiful. I sense God embracing me in love, even when I do not like myself. I am accepted just as I am; I am lovingly lured beyond who I am. I hear God inviting me to be co-creator to enrich the world. I walk with a fellow adventurer in a journey which never ends.

I practice certain spiritual disciplines which grow out of this knowing. I remind myself of how the Caring Friend embraces the world. I watch for, listen for, and feel for new direction, which comes in so many surprising and mysterious ways. I raise a question with myself in important moments:

Who does God want me to be here? I let important decisions simmer and incubate.

I evaluate new direction by comparing it to tradition, weighing its effect on me and the world about me, and estimating how it will affect the future me and the future world, both of which I can see only dimly. I rehearse major steps before taking them. I name the peace which I experience as God's presence, and I value every small act which I perform because I know it is meaningful to God.

These understandings and spiritual practices have enriched my relationship with God. Neither is complete, for I still adventure in both understanding and practice. Much is left unfinished, but adventures are made of such incompleteness. So, I invite you to enter the adventure. I hope that you are led to further inquiring, searching, and risking.

I am curious about your responses as you have read this book. Reading has often been compared to the reader having a conversation with the author. If so, I can imagine us sitting together by the fireplace in our comfortable chairs. In this setting I will be able to express my curiosity directly as I am sure that you have been raising questions with me.

If what I presented about myself struck a chord in you, then we have a common bond. If, however, you found my experiences strange and puzzling, then you have already begun to identify those aspects of you which are clearly different from me. Alike or different, in your response to me you have learned about yourself.

So I am curious about the voices that speak within you when you face a major decision, or for that matter, even a small one. I wonder who serves as chairperson when you stand at a crossroad. Likewise, knowing the pain of losing my mother, I wonder if you have lost one or more significant persons in your life. I want to ask how your understanding of

God helped or hindered you in the labored steps of coming to terms with your loss.

Now you know that a prominent part of me has been the coward, and I am wondering how you labeled yourself in childhood. You may have made that powerful decision in your teenage years. Whenever the labeling occurred, if your earlier choice was a limiting or destructive one, I hope that you have been aware of God calling you to rename yourself.

Some have been known to laugh in disbelief when I tell them of the trials and tribulations that I go through when I pick up a menu. Gradually, I have come to accept my "menu trauma." But then, perhaps you go through a similar struggle or maybe you usually know before you are seated what you will order for lunch. Whichever is true, the valuable information is to know the names of those who guide you in those moments. Similar to mine or different from mine, the key is to know who is speaking.

I have never been a habitual smoker, so I called upon Ann's experience to score my point. Not that I am beyond such frustrating habits, for I could have used my lifelong experience as a fingernail biter. As we visit together, I wonder if you have habits which have been with you for as long as you can remember.

Such habits can be gold mines in which to dig for the prompting of God and important testing grounds for God's rich offering of who you might become. It is my hope that my experience as coward and Ann's experience with smoking might offer hope for you in daring to make those changes which you deeply desire.

Few areas of my life have brought me more joy and depression than that of being a parent. Marge represents both myself and many others with whom I have consulted through the years. I am wondering if you have been searching for new approaches to parenting which leave both you and your children feeling better. So often we identify control and strictness as love, listening and persuasion as weak and a lack of caring. In my thinking the Caring Friend image offers a rich reservoir to assist us in parenting. I hope that you will tap that resource.

That which I like the most about this image of God is that it shines new light in so many corners. I do not have to shift gears or use different language when I talk about habits, self-concepts, parenting, Jesus, loss, nuclear holocaust, or death. The image is universal.

Our conversation now leads to my invitation that you seek to answer the unanswered questions and try out the spiritual disciplines for yourself. Indeed, you may be just the one who finds the answer to some difficult question or who discovers by your own practices some new spiritual discipline.

The stage which was set and the dramas which I presented were created to entice you to become actor or actress. I hope that your dramas with the Caring Friend are touching, exciting, and fulfilling.

Dr. Robert Brizee is a United Methodist minister and a counseling psychologist. During his career, he has served several churches in Washington State and California. He and his wife Adrienne currently share a private counseling practice in Wenatchee, Washington.

Robert Brizee has lived in a variety of surroundings during his life: cities, farms, and ranches. This wide body of experiences has given him insight and understanding into how God is able to come into relationship with all people on an individual basis.